HOME GUARD INSTRUCTION, No. 51

BATTLECRAFT AND BATTLE DRILL FOR THE HOME GUARD

PART IV

THE ORGANIZATION OF HOME GUARD DEFENCE

(For issue down to Section Commanders—two copies for each Section.)

(NOTE.—Scale of issue of Part III—2 copies per Section.)

WHERE THIS INSTRUCTION IS AT VARIANCE WITH PREVIOUS HOME GUARD INSTRUCTIONS THIS INSTRUCTION WILL BE ADHERED TO.

Prepared under the Direction of the Commander-in-Chief, Home Forces.

G.H.Q., HOME FORCES,
November, 1943.

CONTENTS.

DIAGRAMS AND ILLUSTRATIONS.

FOREWORD.

Every man in the Home Guard is, to a greater or lesser extent, a specialist. This book does not replace the manuals or other instruction designed to inform on any one subject, be it tactical, administrative, or training. It does attempt to take the pieces, put them together, and present the picture as a whole; a jig-saw puzzle is no longer a puzzle when it has been assembled. The more snugly the pieces fit, the less the cracks will show and the clearer will be the picture.

Every man must know not only his own job, but enough about everyone else's to realise just what is expected of him if the battle comes to Britain.

INTRODUCTION.

Sec. 1. The Plan.

The fighting task of the Home Guard is to deny rail and road communication to the enemy. This will be achieved by defence in depth. The defences consist of a series of localities, mutually supporting whenever possible, and always designed for all-round defence. In invasion the attacking force will probably consist of tanks, infantry (including paratroops) and artillery. Tanks and infantry are not road-bound, but artillery and supply columns are. Tanks and infantry must be based on roads with uninterrupted service for their supplies. While the Home Guard defended localities control the junctions of communications, the enemy must divert his strength to destroy that defence or risk defeat of his advanced elements through lack of supply.

Equally, if the Home Guard divert their efforts from the operational role assigned to them, it weakens the defence plan which will thus be foredoomed to failure.

Sec. 2. Fighting in towns and villages.

(*a*) *General.* Towns and villages grow round the junctions of the important arteries of communication. The defence of these junctions is the main purpose of most unit defence schemes. Therefore, preparation for fighting in built-up areas is an integral part of most Home Guard training, since they must know how to fight in the houses and factories, in the streets, in the back gardens and yards within and surrounding their defended localities.

(*b*) *Built-up areas favour defence.* It is generally accepted that built-up areas favour the defence. This view is borne out by the fact that the irregularities of pattern of the present day battlefield are largely due to such areas being able to hold out while the attackers progress to considerable distances between and beyond them.

(*c*) *Some aspects of fighting in built-up areas.* The principles of town fighting differ in no way from those which govern more open warfare. There are, however, special circumstances attached to town fighting which have a direct bearing on the tactics employed.

(i) *The ground.* No other battlefield includes ground both so open and so close. In every street are coverless stretches affording ideal fields of fire. Bordering every street are numerous protected firing positions, hiding places, and sources of ambush. It follows that fighting will nearly always be at close quarters, casualties high, and the nerve strain for both sides heavy.

When a built-up area is the scene of a prolonged period of fighting, however, many of its characteristics will be modified. Buildings are liable to become heaps of rubble and fields of view thereby increased. When a whole sector of a town is reduced to rubble, the piles of debris render the area analogous to close country providing much cover; they will also restrict movement, except on foot.

(ii) Built-up areas are usually made up, apart from factories, parks, etc., of three distinct house arrangements: on the outskirts, isolated houses or groups of houses surrounded by gardens, trees, fields and allotments; farther in, closely-spaced detached and semi-detached houses; and, nearest the centre, blocks of houses and large buildings.

(iii) In the area of isolated houses, buildings represent inferior pill-boxes and should be treated as such in attack or defence. Detached and semi-detached jerry-built houses closely spaced are the intermediate stage and are usually flanked by streets on one side and small gardens or back areas on the other. The centre of a town almost invariably consists of buildings built on the block system, so that except for open squares, there is little or no space between them other than that essential for streets and alleyways; but it is important to note that nearly all such buildings have cellars and basements, which assist the defence greatly.

(iv) In densely built-up areas it is possible to climb thirty, fifty, perhaps a hundred feet in as many seconds; it is possible to by-pass an enemy by going directly over or under him. Built-up areas thus possess a third dimension not present in open warfare which, combined with the abundance of cover, involves a constant drain on manpower, creates great difficulties of cohesion and control, and calls for a maximum of ingenuity from everyone engaged.

(v) *Difficulty of control.* Buildings cause exceptionally blind and disjointed conditions. In no other form of warfare, except in dense forest and bush, are there such narrow and limited horizons, or such physical barriers between units of the same force. Highly centralized control will be difficult; most of the fighting will resolve itself into small independent actions, and much will depend upon individual initiative and capabilities. But distances will be short, and therefore will allow commanders to exert a more decisive influence in the local battle because personal appearances well forward in their areas can be made more easily and more quickly than in other forms of fighting.

(vi) *Value of short-range weapons.* Comparison with open warfare brings out the fact that there is a difference in the relative values of the various weapons. AFVs, aircraft and artillery, though invaluable adjuncts, are restricted in their roles; whereas short-range weapons predominate. The psychological effect of noise and fire, especially by night, may often be exploited.

(vii) *Restricted visibility.* Buildings obscure view, and visibility during actual fighting is apt further to be restricted on account of brick dust caused by the strike of projectiles and by explosive charges.

(viii) *Difficulty of locating fire.* The point of origin of fire is made most difficult to locate by reason of the innumerable alternative positions available in houses and the ease with which a sniper or a machine gun can move or be moved from room to room unseen.

(ix) *Restricted manœuvre.* Manœuvre is restricted according to the density of buildings and the nakedness of streets. Success will depend largely upon the judicious variation of method; at one moment stealth and cunning under a small tactical fire plan, at the next the impetus of brute force and speed, for which the qualities of physical fitness and determination to kill are as essential as in open field warfare.

(x) *Value of the first shot.* Fighting is at close quarters, and an aimed shot should be infallibly accurate. Neutralization of fire has, therefore, to be absolute, and covering fire is essential for the smallest operation. A single marksman left undisturbed may be able to prevent any small tactical operation

(xi) The enemy's fire can be stopped by ours in two main ways: either by getting in the first accurate shot, or by getting in more shots, and from more directions, than the enemy can. The first is preferable and saves valuable lives, but, to obtain it, observation by every man in an organized system must be taught

(xii) *Darkness.* Owing to the restriction of movement outside buildings by day much fighting in towns will take place at night. Streets can be crossed, small parties can stalk past defended houses, and it will be difficult to distinguish between friend and foe. Darkness is the ally of the attacker rather than of the defence.

(xiii) *Fire (the element).* Fires can be a formidable and disconcerting agent and is a potent factor in town fighting. A German manual states that " the burning of houses will hasten success," and it is indeed obvious that situations will arise in which the quickest, surest, most economical and perhaps the only way of dislodging the enemy from a building will be by burning it. In defence, precautions against fire should be given high priority to ensure that the work of fortifying buildings is not undone by the first incendiary projectile

Used intentionally, fires produced by one's own side have a very heartening influence and a proportionately depressing effect upon the enemy. Nevertheless, clear orders concerning the use of incendiarism are always necessary because it is a double-edged weapon, which can do more harm than good.

(xiv) *Importance of height.* The possession of height gives a feeling of security over an enemy who is on a lower level, but is often counterbalanced by the effect of hostile air-bombing, which will generally accompany the attack or defence of urban areas.

The defender, who has usually had time to conceal and protect his fire points and to guard all approaches to his level from heights above, will usually prefer to employ his fire raking the streets and lower storeys, feeling that if buildings collapse from shelling and bombing, the rubble, etc., will strengthen his cover and block the streets, thereby giving him increased security and better targets. The attacker, however, will require height to act as depth to his fire support and to assist his observation. The defender knows this fact and will arrange to meet it. The use of available high buildings may, against a well-equipped army prove over-expensive except for sniper and observation posts : and better progress in the attack and greater effect of fire in the defence may be produced by action in and through lower storeys and basements. The shape of roofs and the facilities for reaching them are very important factors in these considerations.

Sec. 3. Principles of Home Guard defence.

The principles that must govern the design of the defence plan and its successful operation are seven. They must be intelligently applied to the ground, be it open or close, town or country.

(*a*) *Defence is final.* A defended locality must fight to the last man and last round.

(*b*) *Defended localities must be sited in depth.* The enemy may infiltrate between localities, he may overrun one, but the impetus will be slowed down as he advances and he can be dealt with by vigorous counter-attack.

(*c*) *All-round defence.* Every defended position, large or small, must be sited for all-round defence.

(*d*) *Aggressive defence.* Defence must not be static. Every commander must have his mobile reserve to dominate his front by fighting patrols and snipers and to destroy the enemy by counter-attack.

(*e*) *Defence must be concentrated:* Seeds, not soldiers, survive distribution in penny packets. It is fire power that stops an attack. Keep the size of a locality small enough to produce concentrated weapon fire. Defend essentials only.

(*f*) *Mutual support.* Enfilade fire by machine guns and A-tk weapons is more effective than frontal fire. It often assists concealment. It allows one locality or strongpoint to support the neighbouring ones.

(*g*) *Concealment is paramount.* A post located can often be neutralized. A vital element in successful defence is surprise. Conceal yourself, your positions, your weapons. Don't let the enemy draw your fire. Hold it till he attacks in force.

CHAPTER I.

THE ORGANIZATION OF DEFENCE.

Sec. 4. Administrative and battle sub-units.

The role of the Home Guard is limited to the defence of its own area. Its degree of mobility is confined to movement within that area. Too direct a comparison with the Field Force or imitation of its tactics and organization should not be attempted. The Home Guard organization has been kept as flexible as possible so that the operational and administrative problems of each locality can be solved by adapting the size of units and the variety of weapons issued to local requirements. It is, however, obviously desirable that, whenever possible, the administrative company and platoon should be the same as the operational equivalent.

Sec. 5. Some definitions.

1. *A defended area.* A defended area consists of a group of defended localities. The defence scheme often permits of enemy penetration into the area between the defended localities with a view to entrapping the attackers and destroying them by fire and counter-attack.

2. *A defended locality* consists of squad and platoon posts each capable of all-round defence and mutually supporting. The whole to be strong, independent and self-supporting. Any infiltration into the defended locality must be destroyed by fire and counter-attack.

One or more companies can form a defended locality, and a defended area will seldom be less than a battalion.

3. *The Keep.* The inner and ultimate defence of any defended area or locality which will contain the military and civil defence headquarters.

4. *Platoon and squad posts* are sub-divisions within the defended locality, themselves sited for all-round defence, and each with its own reserve.

5. *A battle platoon* is the smallest sub-unit commanded by an officer and consists of two or more squads. As, however, control must be by voice or orderly it should not consist of more than four squads. Generally a Battle Platoon HQ should consist of Pl. Comd., Pl. Sjt, 1 rifleman bomber, 1 sniper and 1 runner.

6. *A squad* should usually consist of not less than one NCO and seven men. (*See* also Home Guard Instruction No. 51, Part I, Sec. 1.)

7. *2 pr., sub-artillery and machine gun detachments.* These detachments consist of one NCO and appropriate crew and are attached

to battle platoons or higher formations as the senior commander may direct.

Sec. 6. Defended areas.

1. The formation of defended areas containing a group of defended localities is only justified where Field Force units or mobile units (or sub-units) of the Home Guard are available and trained for a counter-attack role. In these cases the commander and his headquarters are part of the Regular Army, and their organization does not come within the scope of this Instruction.

2. The organization of defended areas is often necessary for the defence of large towns. A town with a total area of one square mile has a perimeter of approximately four miles, and the area enclosed by a long perimeter would require prohibitive numbers of troops to provide depth everywhere. The problem is aggravated by the fact that restricted fields of fire prevent mutual support except from positions much closer together than in normal open country. It will be necessary, therefore, to concentrate on the defence of selected parts of built-up areas, such as the main routes into them and key points which are well adapted for defence, and which it is vital to deny to the enemy. Each of these localities will provide a pivot upon which the mobile elements can act offensively. These mobile elements will be drawn mainly from the area reserve. (*See* also Sec. 10, para. 1 (*b*)—Mobile Home Guard battalions and companies.)

Sec. 7. Defended localities.

1. **The Keep.** Every defended locality should have as its centre a strongpoint or keep containing the headquarters. In it, or very near to it, must be located the commander's main reserve. Once the battle is joined the Force commander can influence its progress only by the use of this reserve. The keep must have its own all round defences. These defences will include prepared positions for the reserve in their secondary role—that is when not employed on patrols or counter-attack. *The keep is not a sort of inner position to which squad posts retire. The enemy must be kept out of every squad post of the defended locality. Each post must be defended to the last man and the last round.* The main purpose of the keep is a secure base for counter-attack. It is therefore only incidental that the keep will be the last place holding out if the whole locality is overrun by insuperable numbers. Usually a defended locality is designed to deny communications to the enemy. If possible therefore the keep should be so placed that it will continue to do this even if the rest of the locality is overrun.

2. **Headquarters.** If the commander is to know when and where

to commit his reserve he must have all possible information passed rapidly and accurately to his headquarters from all posts and patrols.

The layout and organization of a battalion headquarters is in Chapter III (*see* also Fig. 4).

3. **Civil Defence.** The headquarters of a defended locality should be as near as possible to the civil defence headquarters. The Home Guard in most localities depend largely on the civil defence organization for :—

(*a*) Additional labour to complete defences after "ACTION STATIONS."
(*b*) Clearing people from houses required for the defence, or to be demolished to improve fields of fire, etc.
(*c*) Repair of roads damaged by enemy action.
(*d*) Water supplies (normal and emergency)
(*e*) Evacuation of wounded.
(*f*) Feeding and cooking.
(*g*) Fire fighting.
(*h*) Decontamination

Equally, the Home Guard (if not under immediate threat of enemy attack) may have to help the civil defence in controlling fires, traffic control, evacuation of civilians, first aid and rescue work.

The civil defence organization has a complete system of telephone communication and reporting centres of its own. The interchange of information must be absolute. Closest co-operation between the military and civil headquarters is essential.

The German methods of total war against soldier and civilian alike can only be defeated by total defence. The civil defence organization is there, use it and give it all assistance.

4. **The Reserve.** The Force commander's reserve will have as its primary role patrolling, sniping and counter-attack. It must, however, have its own prepared defensive positions.

Figs. 1 and 2 give examples of the layout of a company locality in the town and country

Points to note in Fig. 1

1. The reserve platoon, although sited for defence, is not essential for the company fire plan.

2. The fields of fire indicated above do not include tasks for mutual support between squads. These tasks are part of each platoon fire plan.

3. The triangular block (E) contains no posts. It is within the company killing ground. Any enemy attempting to gain access to

THE LAYOUT OF A COMPANY LOCALITY IN A TOWN

LEGEND

	Platoon Position
	Company H.Q.
	Road-Block.
A	Block of buildings, containing the reserve platoon.
B	Blocks of buildings, containing a platoon and company H.Q.
C & D.	Blocks of buildings, containing a platoon

FIG. 1

it will come under fire from two platoon posts. Those who successfully penetrate this fire will be counter-attacked, first by fire, including EY rifle and sub-artillery, and if necessary, by the reserve platoon.

4. All roads leading into the locality are blocked. Blocks are so constructed as to allow free movement of our own troops and transport.

Sec. 8. The battle platoon position.

1. General.

(*a*) *In the country.* The area to be held must not be too large. 100 square yards is the maximum that three squads can defend and be under the control of the platoon commander. Besides, wider dispersion means fire power will be ineffective.

If the platoon strongpoint is less than 50 yards square there is no room to manœuvre, and neutralization by fire (from the air, artillery, mortar or machine guns) is made easy.

(*b*) *In towns.* In towns these dimensions do not hold good. Usually the main killing grounds will be streets and small open spaces interspersed with blocks of buildings through which the enemy cannot make rapid progress if these approaches are adequately guarded by snipers and OPs and fighting patrols.

The battle platoon position will usually be sited in a block of houses built round a central court or well. The ground for manœuvre will be the houses themselves and in the central court. Complete freedom of movement must be obtained by knocking holes in walls. All entrances to the defended locality must be closed with the most effective type of obstacle.

2. Siting squad posts. The position will consist of a group of squad posts sited to conform to the seven principles of defence laid down in the Introduction, Sec. 3. More often than not these principles are competitive or conflicting. The skill of the good commander is shown in how he makes his choice, valuing the relative importance of each factor and making the most practical compromise.

Thus :—

Concealment must not be disregarded for ideal field of fire or field of view.

To obtain the advantage of some natural obstacle, neither mutual support, control, nor field of fire must be sacrificed. All platoon posts must be able to bring flanking fire in support of their neighbours. Often fields of view and fields of fire can be artificially improved ; most natural obstacles can be improved and strengthened.

The methods of defence and the work to be done vary between

THE LAYOUT OF A COY LOCALITY IN THE COUNTRY

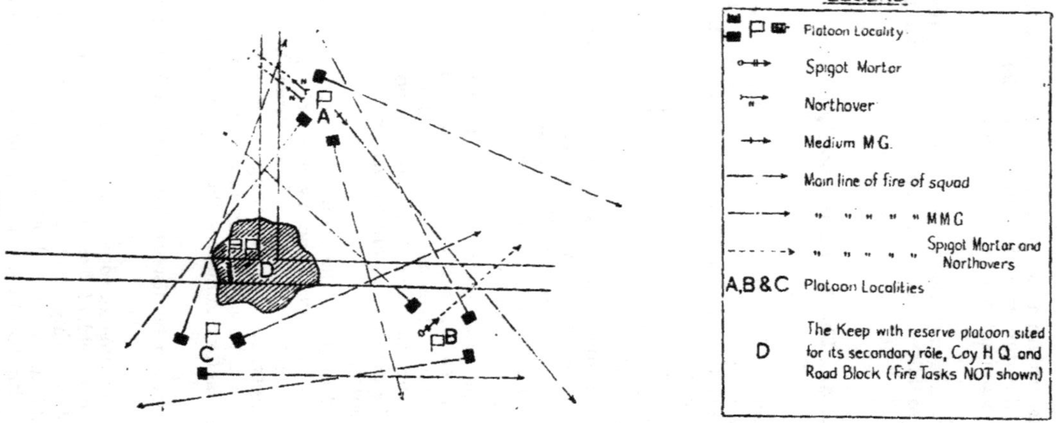

NOTE:- Primary Fire Tasks only are shown for the sake of clarity.
Secondary Fire Tasks for mutual support of squads within platoons are NOT shown.

FIG. 2.

town and country. Both aspects are dealt with in Appendix A and FSPB Part I, Pamphlet No. 7 (in course of preparation).

3. Siting of platoon and squad posts in country and towns. Platoon localities and squad posts in the country will nearly always be under cover in slit trenches or weapon pits. Isolated houses should not form part of the defence as they are an easy mark for enemy fire. In towns, however, the defence will largely be in houses.

(*a*) Select well-built houses for platoon headquarters and squad posts. (*See* Figs. 13 and 14 and Appendix A.)

(*b*) Put snipers and observers on the roofs or in the attics to get the best field of fire and field of view, and to prevent enemy roof-top attack.

(*c*) Put bombers on upper floors to drop or throw the appropriate grenade on the attackers in the killing ground.

(*d*) Put the MG and BAR group on the ground floor to obtain grazing fire, with alternative positions in neighbouring houses and on the first floor in case the enemy gain a temporary foothold in the ground floor. Remaining riflemen should be similarly sited.

(*e*) Where cover from view and suitable fields of fire exist, slit trenches and weapon slits should be prepared near the defended house.

(*f*) Use cellars and basements as headquarters, a gas-proof room (for a HQ), rest rooms and store rooms for ammunition, food and water. Always have two exits. If there is only one, make another.

4. The platoon reserve. The platoon commander must organize a reserve of fire power. Whenever possible this should consist of a complete squad. If a squad cannot be withdrawn to form the reserve, an extra squad can be formed from the reserves of 3 men in each squad (*See* Home Guard Instruction No. 51, Part I, Sec. 1) under command of the platoon serjeant or other available NCO.

5. The squad post.

(*a*) Each squad must know its function within the platoon position and constant touch must be kept with platoon headquarters and neighbouring squads.

Defence works are never complete and more than one position for each squad post must be prepared.

(*b*) *Road-blocks.* Every road leading into a defended locality must be guarded. Part of the defence of the road will be a road-block. Often a pill-box has been constructed. The duties of squads, machine gun and sub-artillery detachments, assigned to road defence are dealt with in Chapter IV.

6. Alternative positions. The use of alternative positions is sometimes misunderstood. Their purpose is not to serve as a refuge when the garrison of a post or locality is hard pressed by the engaging enemy or is heavily bombarded.

Alternative positions are required for the following purposes :—

(*a*) To meet necessary variations in day and night dispositions.

(*b*) To meet the requirements of alternative tasks or a temporary change in role, eg to cover another area ; to support a counter-attack ; or to achieve surprise.

(*c*) To mystify the enemy as to the position and strength of the defence, by occupying positions in rotation.

(*d*) For occupation, should a building, which forms a defended post, be burnt out.

(*e*) Where a position has become heavily contaminated by blister gas.

Sec. 9. Around and about the defended locality.

1. Information, observation and reporting. The commander of a defended locality will always attempt to dominate the ground on his immediate front. To do this he requires early and accurate information of the enemy's movements. *He will use the information for the intelligent direction of his fighting patrols, and can harass the enemy with well-placed snipers.*

It cannot be emphasized enough that early and accurate information of enemy movements is vital to successful operations by mobile reserves outside the defended locality.

This information can be obtained by reconnaissance patrols, standing patrols and OPs.

The Force commander may also receive reports of enemy movement affecting his area from higher headquarters ; obtained by air reconnaissance, or through the intelligence service. It is essential that information obtained from all forward elements be immediately passed back to the next higher headquarters so as to reach the intelligence officers whose duty it is to use it to corroborate and add to information obtained from other sources.

As in all military problems a commander must strike a balance between troops used for information and troops used for fighting. The commander will wish to supplement intelligence he may receive from higher headquarters, and will be expected to do so regarding all events in his sector of responsibility. This *must not*, however, be taken to such lengths as to exhaust, from lack of sleep, men who will be required for the fight.

Therefore, each standing patrol and OP will usually be authorized by the Force commander, and OPs manned with personnel directly at the disposal of the battalion intelligence officer. They will, of course, be in touch with squad posts in the section of the perimeter they are watching.

2. **Standing patrols.** Standing patrols are seldom employed for observation only. They usually have sufficient fire power to cause the enemy to deploy prematurely. They must not get so involved with the enemy attack that they have to be extricated. Therefore their orders as to withdrawal must be clear. On withdrawal they once more become part of the reserve. (*See* also Home Guard Instruction No. 51, Part III, Sec. 12.)

3. **OPs.** The necessity for numerous OPs in town fighting has been made clear in the Introduction. They are more readily organized in towns as their positions are easily concealed, and a covered method of approach and get-away is easily devised.

In rural districts also, there are frequently areas not covered from view from any platoon position which it may be essential for tactical reasons to have under observation. If these OPs are to be manned for any length of time—or permanently after "ACTION STATIONS" —they must be carefully constructed and concealed ; the covered approach reconnoitred and rigid track discipline maintained. Under these conditions no OP can be manned by less than one NCO and six men, and all arrangements must allow for this. (*See* Appendix B on Organization of OPs.)

4. **Reconnaissance patrols.** These patrols are usually sent out with a specific mission—to confirm or disprove information received —to obtain details of the enemy's position with a view to attack. Their route, time of departure and return must be given them, and all squad posts, OPs and standing patrols affected informed. The defended locality commander must, therefore, normally decide whether they shall be found from his own reserve or that of some sub-unit.

5. **Snipers.** The number of snipers that each unit or sub-unit should train must depend on the operational role.

The Home Guard possess no snipers' rifles as an official issue, but the ·300 or ·303 rifle is an accurate weapon up to 400 yards in the hands of the well-trained sniper.

The sniper must be highly skilled in battlecraft and get used to working on his own or at most with one observer. His operations must be governed by the defence plan so that, for instance, he is not sited near an OP. If he is, he may draw hostile fire on it and the discharge of his rifle may interfere with the OP hearing enemy movements.

Snipers form a very important part of the defence in towns. Properly disposed they can have a devastating effect upon the enemy approach and morale.

Streets and open spaces will be covered by squad posts armed with machine guns, automatics and sub-artillery detachments. The approaches over roof tops and through houses will be protected by snipers.

A sniper can conceal himself by placing himself as far back in the room as the required field of fire permits.

Loop-holes are easily made by knocking out a brick from a wall or slates from roofs. The loop-hole in use may be disguised by making false ones around it.

Hitherto the full use of snipers has not been exploited in Home Guard defence schemes largely because of the shortage of training ammunition. This is no longer the case and battalion commanders must consider the number of snipers required for their operational role, and train them. (*See* also M.T.P. No. 44—Notes on the Training of Snipers, Home Guard Instruction No. 49 and Home Guard Information Circular No. 24, para. 7—·303 " Small Mark " Practice Ammunition.)

6. **Fighting Patrols.** Fighting patrols will be the most usual forces employed by the locality commander to dominate the ground immediately outside the perimeter of his defences. Their operation and training are discussed in Home Guard Instruction No. 51, Part III, Sec. 11.

Sec. 10. The fighting troops outside the defended locality.

1. The fighting troops that may be operating against the enemy outside the defended locality may consist of :—

(*a*) *The Field Force.* Their action will be largely independent of the Home Guard who will receive information of their intentions from higher headquarters.

These troops will often be without detailed information of the neighbourhood other than that they obtain from their maps. The Home Guard can give them important assistance by providing guides and information about the enemy's movements.

(*b*) *Mobile Home Guard battalions and companies.* As described in Sec. 6 the defence plan may be organized into a defended area permitting enemy infiltration between the defended localities. Mobile Home Guard battalions and companies are provided with motor transport to bring them quickly to the necessary concentration point for counter-attack. These units should not be employed outside the areas which they know thoroughly and where they have been trained *on the ground* for all possible operations in which they are likely to be employed.

The fact that they are provided with motor transport must under no circumstances make them round-bound or so minded. They must consist of active men well trained in battlecraft and able to attack in town or country or both, according to their operational role.

All must be trained in road discipline and the protection of motor transport *en route* and when parked.

They will often be armed with A-tk rifles, 3-inch OSB guns and 2-pr A-tk guns. The tactical handling of these weapons must be part of the training of the commanders and the crews.

(*c*) *Isolated sub-units.*

(i) *General.* It has been laid down that a defended locality shall consist of not less than one battle platoon for defences and one battle platoon in reserve (a platoon to consist of not less than three squads and platoon headquarters). Isolated units below this strength will therefore be allotted other roles. These roles must, however, form an integral part of the defence organization of the area in which they will operate. *There is no room in modern war for uncontrolled bodies of men wandering about the country imagining they are doing guerilla fighting, demolishing communications essential in the counter-attack, and being as much danger to our own fighting patrols as to the enemy's.*

In some places these platoons form part of the mobile reserve of a neighbouring defended locality. In this case their duties have been dealt with in preceding sections, since they form part of the reserve within a defended locality.

Elsewhere such isolated sub-units will be given specific roles of observation, reporting and harassing the enemy outside the perimeter of defended localities.

(ii) *Observation and reporting*. Every individual must be highly trained in battlecraft. The platoon headquarters relies on concealment only against capture. Its position therefore must be dictated by the movements of the enemy and alternative hide-outs must be prepared and known to all.

From these headquarters methods to keep intercommunication with the headquarters of the nearest defended locality must be planned and tried out under every likely eventuality. Observing is valueless without reporting. Reporting requires communications.

If the role of the sub-unit is limited by the higher commander to observing, all offensive action that will make the enemy suspect that they are under observation must be avoided. The temptation to pick off the odd man or the odd staff car may prevent the scouts passing back information ; locating an important headquarters or enemy concentration that can be effectively dealt with by concentrated artillery fire or air bombardment. The less the enemy even suspect the presence of hostile patrols, the more can information be obtained and rapidly communicated to information centres.

(iii) *Harassing tactics*. The military situation may require that these isolated platoons should also adopt harassing tactics which in broken or close country can be most disruptive to the enemy's communications and force him to detach troops from the main attack to guard vital lines of supply.

There must be constant communication and cooperation with the headquarters of defended areas or localities, so that the activities of these mobile fighting patrols can be part of the offensive defence, and so that all information obtained reaches higher headquarters.

Snipers, tip-and-run ambushes, attacks on tanks in harbour and on isolated units must be the methods employed.

Through their intimate knowledge of the ground they will know where to strike. Through accurate observing they will know when. Through training they will know how. Observe, plan, strike, withdraw. Re-organize and repeat the process somewhere else.

(iv) *Administration*. These platoons, while outside the perimeter must be part of the plan of the defended area or locality upon which they will be based for communication and supply. It must be remembered that they cannot rely on living on the country for food. For the enemy may sweep it bare. In any event they will rely on their base for ammunition supply even if this can be supplemented by captures from the enemy.

Sec. 11. Summary.

The above is a picture of the organized defence from the keep with its headquarters to the outer perimeter, and of the troops that will be in action outside each defended locality.

The keep with its headquarters is the nerve centre with absolute control of the reserve for the counter-attack. The platoon positions and their squad posts surround it and its defences. Outside these posts, covering the ground where the enemy must deploy, are a network of information points to direct the fighting patrols and snipers. Beyond these again may be the special units helping the defences with information and others employed on major counter-attack measures.

The whole system of defended areas and localities covering Great Britain constitutes defence in depth taken to finality.

CHAPTER II.

THE FIRE PLAN.

Sec. 12. General.

It is bullets and projectiles that will halt or break up the enemy attack. Therefore the commander must know the characteristics of every Home Guard weapon with which his unit or sub-unit is armed so that he can site them to the best advantage.

Sec. 13. Characteristics of Home Guard weapons.

For convenience, a short summary of the characteristics and tactical handling of these weapons is given below.

1. Small Arms.

(*a*) *Ranges*. The maximum ranges at which Home Guard small arms are to be used have been limited largely because of the shortage of training ammunition. This no longer exists and the ranges which experience in the various campaigns of this war has shown to be useful are now authorized for Home Guard. These ranges are :—

	Maximum.	*Best.*
Rifles and Browning Automatics	400 yards	200 yards.
Stens	50 ,,	10–20 yards.
Revolvers	40 ,,	15 yards.
Shotguns	40 ,,	20 ,,
LMG and MMGs.	500 ,,	200–300 yards.

(*b*) *The rifle.* Flat trajectory up to 400 yards. Good accuracy in hands of well-trained man.

Tactical use. To fill the gaps in the killing ground not fully covered by MMGs and LMGs. To arm the battle platoon as laid down in Home Guard Instruction No. 51, Part II, Sec. 5. To arm snipers.

(*c*) *Browning Automatic.* As for the rifle, except that its fire is more rapid than rifle fire, so that it is a waste of fire power to give it to a sniper.

(*d*) *Stens.* A light handy weapon with a high rate of fire and accuracy at short ranges.

Tactical use. The use of the Sten may be likened to an extended bayonet. To arm the battle platoon as laid down in Home Guard Instruction No. 51, Part II, Sec. 5. To protect sub-artillery and MMG positions. To arm DRs and Home Guard MT companies.

(*e*) *Shotguns.* An effective man-killing short range weapon. Three types of shot are issued—SG, LG and Lethal ball.

Lethal ball will kill at longer ranges, but does not have the advantage of SG or LG shot with a spread of approximately 3 feet diameter at 40 yards and 1 foot at 20 yards. SG shot will penetrate a car windscreen of triplex glass at 40 yards.

Tactical handling. These spreads with SG and LG make the shotgun a peculiarly suitable and effective weapon for night patrols, and ambushes. By day it may be used to supplement the close range defence of sub-artillery positions.

(*f*) *Revolvers.* Short range rapid fire. Only accurate in hands of an experienced shot.

Tactical handling. To arm battle platoons as laid down in Home Guard Instruction No. 51, Part II, Sec. 5. To arm officers and DRs (if they prefer revolvers to Stens).

(*g*) *MMGs and LMGs.* These guns have the highest sustained rate of fire of any weapons with which the Home Guard is armed. The effective beaten zone of the bullets is long and narrow. MMGs are not very mobile. LMGs are more so, but both weapons are best reserved for the defences of the localities ; light automatics being used for patrols.

Tactical handling. MMGs and LMGs should be sited to fire enfilade so that the maximum number of the attackers will be within the beaten zone in any one burst. They are less easy to conceal than rifles and automatics, so should, when possible, be defiladed from the enemy.

2. Artillery and sub-artillery.

(*a*) *Ranges.* These weapons are issued primarily as anti-tank defence and attack, although some of them have anti-personnel ammunition as well. The effective ranges of these weapons are :—

	Maximum.	*Best.*
Northover Projector using :—		
68 grenade	60 yards	50 yards.
76 SIP grenade	120 „	70 „
36 grenade—		
4 sec. fuze	150 „	—
7 sec. fuze	200 „	—
29-mm. Spigot Mortar :—		
20 lb. HE anti-tank	200 „	100 yards.
14 lb. HE anti-personnel	750 „	400 „
3-inch OSB Gun :—		
8 lb. HE anti-personnel	650 „	150 „
6 lb. HE anti-tank	200 „	100 „
2-pr., armour-piercing shot	500 „	200 „

(*b*) *Protection.* When used as part of the defences of a locality, they must always be sited inside the infantry defences and afforded small arms protection.

(*c*) *The Northover Projector.* A short range weapon from which No. 68 grenades, No. 76 grenades (SIP) and No. 36 grenades 4 sec. or 7 sec., can be fired. Firing the No. 68 grenade it can destroy light tanks and damage heavy ones, with a direct hit on track or bogies. Firing the No. 76 grenade it can complete the destruction of a tank brought to a halt and force the crew to dismount. SIPs can be fired into windows of defended houses to smoke out the garrison. It will almost certainly set the house on fire. Firing the No. 36 grenade, the projector can be used in any suitable anti-personnel role.

It is fairly mobile for short distances, the barrel and mounting being manhandled by two men. The gun can be fired with reasonable accuracy without its mounting, but resting on cover. Used thus, it of course acquires much greater mobility.

Tactical handling. Primarily an ambush anti-tank weapon to be sited as part of the defences to fire enfilade on likely tank approaches. As it is easily transported a commander can allot a projector and its detachment to a standing patrol needing additional anti-tank defence. A secondary role is to search for enemy under cover from view or small enemy concentrations. For this purposes it fires No. 36 grenades at a range to ensure a low air burst. Another use is in support of an attack on a defended house. The SIP on bursting emits a good deal of smoke. Under favourable circumstances an effective smoke screen can be created. It must be remembered the smoke has toxic properties so it should not be so used if our own men will remain long in it.

(*d*) *29-mm. Spigot Mortar.* In its primary role firing a 20 lb. HE anti-tank bomb, a direct hit will almost certainly severely damage, if not destroy, any heavy tank now known. In its secondary role, firing 14 lb. HE anti-personnel bombs, the danger area is 100 yards radius from the point of impact of the bomb. It is a low muzzle (or spigot) velocity weapon which gives considerable variations of trajectory at long and short ranges. For instance, the top of the trajectory firing the anti-personnel bomb is 26 feet at 200 yards and 285 feet at 500 yards. The mortar has a portable and a fixed mounting, but no great degree of mobility. While fairly easily camouflaged (*see* Appendix E), it can be quickly spotted and neutralized once it has come into action.

Tactical handling. This most destructive of all the Home Guard anti-tank weapons should be used primarily as a short range anti-tank weapon firing enfilade at main tank approaches from defiladed positions. Only when all these approaches are well covered by anti-tank weapons should it be employed in an anti-personnel role. It must be remembered that the mortar has a slow rate of fire compared to the opposing tank. Its object must be to get in its first shot at a previously registered range to destroy the opposing AFV before it can open fire. If the tanks retire (apart from any knocked out) the opportunity should be seized to move to the alternative prepared position. It will be realised that the element of surprise essential to success will be lost if the mortar is first used on anti-personnel targets at longer ranges. It will be neutralized or knocked out before the tanks advance. Where one or more mortars can be spared from the anti-tank role to fill the anti-personnel role, they should be used for likely enemy infantry approaches to thicken-up the fire in the killing ground. Also they can be used to cover enemy assembly positions.

Counter-attack. The Spigot Mortar sited to the flank of a locality overrun by the enemy, can support a counter-attack using anti-personnel bombs.

(*e*) *3-inch OSB Gun* (*Smith Gun*). The gun is a mobile weapon which can fire anti-tank or anti-personnel shells. The anti-tank bomb will pierce 80 mm. of armour plate at 50 yards. It will penetrate ferro-concrete and brick walls 9 inches thick, making a hole about 2 feet in diameter.

The danger area from the point of burst is 300 yards with the anti-tank bomb. The anti-personnel shell has a danger area of 100 yards radius from point of burst. Both have a low trajectory, so that a low wall 3 feet high necessitates the gun being sited about 20 yards behind it. It is not easy to conceal.

Tactical handling. *In defence* the anti-personnel shell should be used to cover dead ground by either direct or indirect fire, the gun can be fired off any sort of ground provided the wheel base is roughly level. Owing to difficulties of concealment, alternative positions should be selected and prepared. Covered routes to the positions must be reconnoitred. Whenever possible, the trailer should be left in a central position from which both the original and the alternative positions can be fed.

In reserve the gun can be retained by the Force commander with the reserve to reinforce any threatened locality with minimum delay. It is very mobile and can be towed behind a 10 h.p. car, or a motor cycle.

In counter-attack the gun can support infantry with fire from a flank. It can be used to dislodge enemy established in a building. Having wheels, it is more suitable than the Northover for use with standing patrols. At Appendix D are some notes resulting from trials of the gun with live ammunition in a built-up area.

(*f*) *The 2-pr*. The 2-pr is an accurate and quick-firing A-tk weapon with a flat trajectory. It is small and easily concealed. It can be manhandled and towed on the road behind any vehicle capable of carrying the crew of four and a supply of ammunition. The maximum range at which fire will be opened is 500 yards, but the best range is 200 yards.

Tactical handling. In view of its longer range, the primary use of the 2-pr is to cover likely tank and soft vehicle approaches to the defensive locality which are beyond the range of the Home Guard sub-artillery weapons. It may also be used as a reserve A-tk weapon in the hands of a commander to destroy any tanks which may penetrate his locality, and to replace any anti-tank weapons which may have been overrun.

3. **The cup discharger and the A-tk rifle.** These two weapons do not fall within the classification of paras. 1 and 2.

(*a*) *The cup discharger*. The EY rifle with cup discharger can fire No. 68 grenades or No. 36 grenades. The ranges with the No. 68 grenade are 50–75 yards. The trajectory of the No. 68 grenade is such that if it is used at ranges above 75 yards, the grenade will be falling and the fair and square hit necessary to ensure detonation will not be obtained.

The ranges using the No. 36 grenade are :—

With the 4 sec. fuze, the cup discharger should not be used at ranges over 150 yards.

With the 7 sec. fuze, 80 yards with the gas port fully open or all holes uncovered on the No. 2 discharger ; 200 yards with the gas port fully shut or all the holes covered.

Tactical handling. In defence. As an anti-tank or anti-personnel weapon.

In attack. Firing the No. 68 grenade, it is the lightest and handiest anti-tank weapon available to patrols. It may be used to break down barricaded doors, etc., to effect entry into defended houses and in support of the attack. In both attack and defence, the trajectory of the No. 36 grenade fired from the cup discharger enables this weapon to be used to search behind cover.

(*b*) *The anti-tank rifle.* The anti-tank rifle fires a bullet of ·55-in. calibre, and a well-trained man should be able to fire about 9 rounds a minute. This rifle should not be used at ranges above 300 yards.

Tactical handling. The A-tk rifle is *not* effective against heavy armour, and heavier A-tk weapons should be used for this purpose. It can, however, break the tracks of heavy tanks. The bullet can pierce light armour and put soft vehicles out of action. It should be allotted to those parts of the defences where suitable targets are most likely to approach.

4. **Grenades and A-tk mines.** (*See* SAT, Vol. I, Pamphlet 13.) The grenades available for the Home Guard are of two types, anti-personnel and anti-tank.

(*a*) *Anti-personnel.*

(i) *No. 36 Grenade.* An anti-personnel grenade with a 4 sec. or 7 sec. time fuze, weights 1½ lbs., so that the number a man can carry is limited. It has a danger area of 300 yards and must therefore be thrown from behind cover.

Tactical handling. An effective anti-personnel grenade for all types of close-quarter fighting.

(ii) *No. 69 Grenade.* This is a light bakelite grenade exploding on impact. It relies on blast and noise only for its effect. Its " peace-time " danger area is 30 yards.

Tactical handling. To break in light barricades and demoralize the enemy in room to room fighting.

NOTE.—*It is not a general issue, but is found in operational stocks in some localities.*

(*b*) *Anti-tank.*

(i) *No.* 68 *Grenade.* An anti-tank grenade bursting on impact for use with Northover or cup discharger at ranges stated for these weapons.

Tactical handling. For use against light tanks or the tracks and bogies of heavy tanks ; also against soft vehicles. To break down barricades. (*See* also under cup discharger and Northover projector.)

(ii) *No.* 73 *Grenade.* A cylindrical anti-tank grenade weighing 3¾ lbs. exploding on impact.

Tactical handling. For use in ambushes in close-quarter fighting with AFVs from behind cover. Dropped or thrown from windows it will damage a tank turret hit direct.

NOTE.—*This grenade is not now being produced, but can be used where operational stocks exist.*

(iii) *No.* 74 (*ST*) *Grenade.* A glass or bakelite grenade containing a viscous explosive. The bottle is crushed on to a hard surface and the 5 sec. fuze then detonates the grenade, breaching armour plate or walls under the explosive.

Tactical handling. It is best used where the attacker can get right up to the tank to plant the grenade. It will not stick on wet or greasy vertical surfaces, or to plaster. It is a recognized method of demolition.

(iv) *No.* 75 *and* 75*A Grenades.* An anti-tank grenade mine weighing 2½ lbs. It explodes only under compression, and is designed to destroy tank tracks.

Tactical handling. A portable mine to be dug into possible tank approaches. It can be drawn, pushed or thrown immediately in front of an oncoming tank from behind cover (*see* also Home Guard Instruction No. 51, Part III, Sec. 21).

(v) *No.* 76 *SIP Grenade.* This grenade can be used to provide a smoke screen. It can also be used for lobbing through windows either to set fire to a house or smoke out the defenders.

When not fired from a Northover, the bottle may fail to break. Fig. 3 shows one method of ensuring that the grenade explodes.

Sec. 14. The defence scheme.

1. The commander should study the operational role allotted to his unit. Examine the ground he has to defend, then put himself in the place of the enemy and work out all possible approaches and methods of attack, both by AFVs and infantry, by day and by night.

He should list his available weapons and fighting men in terms of sub-units (apart from those who must be detailed for administrative duties).

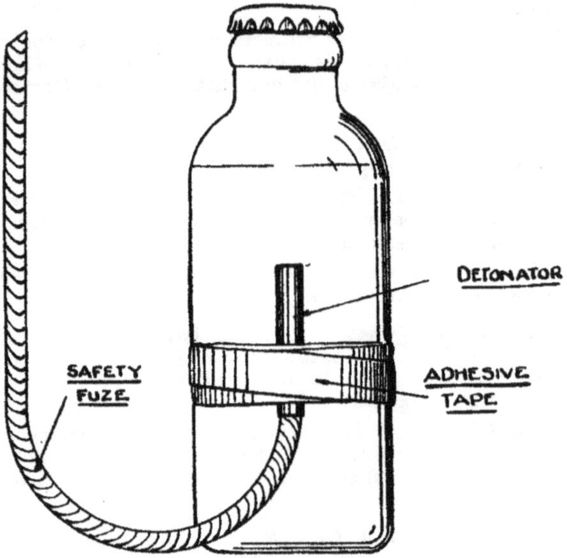

THE S.I.P. GRENADE

WITH DETONATOR ATTACHED.

FIG. 3.

He must next divide his defended locality into sectors in accordance with his appreciation of the possible directions of enemy attack and allot these sectors to his sub-units. The boundaries must be clearly defined and must not be roads or any other main approach to the locality. Having allotted sectors, the commander must then allot his available weapons to sectors in accordance with their characteristics. He must then give each sector its fire task, which will normally be across the front of a neighbouring sector, thus providing mutual support (*see* Figs. 1 and 2).

2. The sub-unit commander will first site his additional weapons in accordance with the plan of his superior commander and then will decide where he must have fire from his small arms to fulfil the task he has been given. When this has been decided, the position of the squad posts will have been fixed, and all that remains is for the final decision to be taken as to the exact positions of weapon pits for forward squads, the platoon reserve and platoon headquarters.

In siting weapons and slit trenches it must be remembered that in the event of invasion, buildings and other obstructions in the fields of fire may be demolished. However, the amount of improvement that can be done will be governed by the time and labour available, so it is best to underestimate.

3. Finally, the complete layout will be re-examined by the commanders concerned in the light of the seven principles of defence (*see* Introduction, Sec. 3), to make sure that it conforms, and that the plan makes the best and correct tactical use of every weapon at the disposal of the force.

Typical layouts are shown in Figs. 1 and 2.

CHAPTER III.

LAYOUT OF A BATTLE HEADQUARTERS.

Sec. 15. General.

1. **Siting.** The position of a battle headquarters will be governed by :—

(*a*) Considerations of defence.
(*b*) A central position.
(*c*) Inter-communication facilities.
(*d*) Co-ordination with Civil Defence.
(*e*) Control of the reserve for counter-attack.
(*f*) Concealment.

The headquarters must be within the keep and usually the reserve will, in its secondary role, have defensive positions guarding the headquarters.

2. **Inter-communication.** The inter-communication system for the Home Guard is laid down in Home Guard Regulations, Vol. II.

The battle headquarters must be sited to make the best use of all methods of communication with sub-units within the defended locality, with higher headquarters and with neighbouring defended localities.

3. **Concealment.** All headquarters will be a first objective of enemy air and artillery attack. So :—

(a) Conceal it from the air.
(b) Enforce track discipline.
(c) Make car parks under trees or camouflage netting. In towns, suitable sheds or garages can be employed.

4. **Alternative headquarters.** After " ACTION STATIONS " an alternative headquarters previously earmarked should be prepared in case the first is destroyed by enemy action. Arrangements must be made to switch over communications without interruption.

5. **Administration.** The preparation of the necessary administrative services after " ACTION STATIONS " is difficult to organize and rehearse beforehand. These services are essential to winning the battle. In organizing a headquarters the necessary personnel and space must be worked out and earmarked.

Sec. 16. Accommodation and equipment.

1. The personnel at a headquarters will be governed by its operational importance and the number of troops it has to administer. Fig. 4 and the notes below show the ideal layout for a battalion headquarters. A company headquarters will usually be much the same on a smaller scale. The commander must decide how much of the personnel, accommodation and equipment he requires.

2. **Room I.** Commanding officer and second in command.

Equipment.
Commander's map with dispositions marked on talc.
Telephone.

Room. II Adjutant and intelligence officer.

Equipment.
Wall-map showing dispositions on talc or with pins.
Battle message board showing all messages received and sent.
Defence plan (sometimes called War Book).
Intelligence log.
Location list.
Telephone.

Room III. Signal officer, clerks and orderlies.

Equipment.
Diagram of signal communication.
Message pads.
Typewriter.
Telephone.

GENERAL LAYOUT OF BATTALION HEADQUARTERS.

FIG. 4.

Room IV. Administrative officer and clerks.

Equipment.
Duty roster for headquarters personnel.
Files to carry out all administrative duties.
Telephone.

3. Rooms I and II should adjoin. Room III should be near entrance to get messages quickly.

Make rooms blast proof by shoring up and sandbagging in front of windows. Arrange for emergency lighting of all rooms. Complete blackout arrangements. Plan method to destroy secret documents quickly.

4. **Marking headquarters.** A board will be painted giving designation of unit or sub-unit and placed where easily seen.

By night an old 4-gallon petrol tin or any other one that suits should be placed over a hurricane lantern. The designation of the unit is cut out of the sides and is easy to see in the dark.

5. **Rest area.** After " ACTION STATIONS " headquarters will be continuously manned.

Arrange adequate accommodation for reliefs off duty to rest and eat. Arrange adequate kitchens and latrines.

Sec. 17. Security.

All headquarters should have a guard.

See also Appendix C for details of duties of sentries.

Sec. 18. Equipment.

1. Below are given some notes on the construction and keeping-up of the equipment detailed in Sec. 16, para. 2.

(*a*) *Battle message board.* Three-ply wood suitably stiffened or other similar substance will make a good message board. Two hooks will be required for each unit or local authority with whom the battalion may interchange messages, one being for messages received and the other for those despatched, ie " IN " and " OUT " messages. An additional hook for multiple addressees " OUT " messages also will be required. The messages can be placed on the board by means of paper clips.

(*b*) *Method of marking.* In every unit each office should have a map. If possible, this map should be in some form of case, whether it be a board covered by talc or something more elaborate. Maps marked in pencil, if they fall into enemy hands will give away information. Marks on talc can be removed more easily and in any case are easier to keep up-to-date.

Maps should be marked as laid down in FSPB Part I, Pamphlet No. 6A.

(c) *Intelligence log.* In order to facilitate easy reference to a message, and to enable the commander or any visitor to obtain a quick idea of events, an intelligence log may be kept at battalion headquarters and at those company headquarters which have an intelligence officer.

This log will be worked in conjunction with the battle message board and it is important for both that a written record of all important telephone messages should be maintained. A pad of suitable paper therefore should be at each telephone, and officers must practise writing down the gist of all conversations they make. These must be timed.

The log should be kept in duplicate, one copy should be hung near the battle message board as each sheet is completed and one retained by the intelligence section. Only essential information and action should be included. The form of this log should be as follows :—

Place................ Sheet No.........

Date................ X Bn. H.G. Intelligence log.

Serial No.	Time	From	To	Event	Action
1.	1015	A Coy	Bn HQ	Enemy infiltration at MILL 091564. Strength 1 Pl.	CO orders D Coy to send fighting patrol.
2.	1030	B Coy	„	Heavy bombing of Station.	Sector HQ informed.
3.	1200	D Coy	„	Enemy referred to in 1 destroyed. 6 casualties.	A Coy informed.
4.	1300	Bn HQ	Police HQ	Suspicious person reported at Gas Works.	Police said they would investigate.

The serial number on the intelligence log should be placed in pencil in the corner of each message before it is filed on the battle message board.

Do not let entering a message in the log delay its receipt by the officer concerned.

Sec. 19. Defence Plan or War Book.

Every defended locality commander must compile one, including a sketch map of the defence layout. It must give details under headings as shown below :—

INFORMATION.	*REMARKS.*
1. Brief description of the locality to be defended, including all special features such as VPs.	
2. Home Guard available for the defence.	Including List i and List ii men specialists weapons, ammunition.
3. Other troops in the neighbourhood.	
INTENTION.	
4. This must state quite clearly the task of the defended locality.	
METHOD.	
5. Division of defended localities into smaller localities and posts with complete fire plan.	Large scale detailed map, showing all defences divided into areas of responsibility.
6. Patrols.	
Details of men allotted for OPs, recce patrols and counter-attack.	This should give full description of the task.
7. Preparation of Defence Works.	
(*a*) Fields of fire to be cleared. (*b*) Slit trenches to be dug.	To be divided into work to be done before and after " ACTION STATIONS." Every defence work, complete or planned, to be given a priority number.
(*c*) Wiring to be completed. (*d*) Buildings to be put in state of defence and order of work. (*e*) Anti-tank minefields to be laid.	

METHOD contd.	*REMARKS.*
(*f*) **Fougasses and flame-throwers.**	
(*g*) Preparation of alternative positions.	
(*h*) Location of defence works stores and where additional stores can be obtained.	
(*j*) Builders or others available to help in work of fortification.	To be agreed with Civil Defence Headquarters.
8. Snipers.	
(*a*) Detail by name.	
(*b*) Positions.	
(*c*) Tasks.	
(*d*) Routes, which can be used under fire.	
9. Road-blocks.	
(*a*) Road-blocks to be manned.	
(*b*) How covered by fire.	
(*c*) Sub-unit responsible.	
(*d*) On whose orders road-blocks are to be placed in position.	
(*e*) Unused—where stored ?	
10. Special duties.	
(*a*) Immobilization of petrol pumps.	
(*b*) Provision of guides.	
(*c*) Protection of VPs.	
(*d*) Establishment of check points.	Only where ordered by higher authority.
ADMINISTRATION.	
11. (*a*) Food.	
(*b*) Cooking and Utensils.	
(*c*) Water.	
(*d*) Pay and Records.	
12. ***Ammunition.***	
(*a*) **Amount to be carried by each man.**	
(*b*) **Reserve—where to be held.**	
(*c*) **Transport arrangements from reserve to squad posts.**	

ADMINISTRATION contd.	*REMARKS.*
13. *Transport.*	
(*a*) Allotment of vehicles.	
(*b*) Earmarked vehicles as arranged with Police.	
(*c*) Supply of petrol.	
(*d*) EL labels.	
14. *Anti-Gas.*	
(*a*) Replacement of respirators.	
(*b*) Decontamination arrangements.	
(*c*) Replacement of contaminated clothing.	
(*d*) Warning signal.	
(*e*) Reporting first use of gas.	
15. *Medical.*	
(*a*) Stretcher bearers and equipment.	
(*b*) Medical supplies.	
(*c*) First Aid posts.	
(*d*) Disposal of casualties.	In conjunction with Civil Defence Headquarters.
(*e*) Sanitary arrangements.	
INTERCOMMUNICATION.	
16. *Methods of communication.*	
(*a*) With higher headquarters.	
(*b*) With lower headquarters.	
(*c*) With neighbouring defended localities.	
(*d*) Between defended locality headquarters and its OPs and patrols.	
(*e*) DRLS system.	

CHAPTER IV.

ROAD-BLOCKS.

Sec. 20. Introduction.

1. No road-block will by itself stop a tank for more than a short time. (*See* films B/C 490, 491, 492.)

However, to destroy an efficient one tanks must stop to reconnoitre. They are then sitting birds and an easy target for A-tk weapons.

Therefore, all important road-blocks should have at least one A-tk weapon sited to a flank to get that tank.

Sec. 21. Offensive Defence.

1. The A-tk crew will require protection from enemy infantry so that at least one squad will be sited round the road-block.

The squad will be ready to destroy any of the tank crew that attempt to get out of the tank. The squad post will be sited for all-round defence. The A-tk. weapon must be sited to fire in any direction. If the ground does not permit this from one position, alternate positions must be prepared to achieve the same object.

2. **Tank tactics.** Tanks seldom advance singly—a troop normally consists of five. They may be preceded or accompanied by reconnaissance cars, motor cyclists or lorried infantry. The column moves when in a danger area by tactical bounds, the tank in rear moving at such a distance that it can support by fire the one in front. When serious opposition is encountered from behind an effective tank obstacle, they will get off the road and try to take cover to reconnoitre for attack. They may cover this movement by smoke. Tanks are highly trained in their own battle drill. The time therefore between sighting the tank and the attack will be short.

Sec. 22. Defence and counter-attack.

1. The force at each road-block must have a defence and counter-attack plan to destroy the maximum amount of the enemy column. This plan will differ with the ground and probable enemy action in each case. (*See* Figs. 5 and 6.)

(*a*) Decide which tank in the column the A-tk weapon will fire at first.

(*b*) If ground permits, have a concealed post from which No. 75 (Hawkins) grenades can be pulled or pushed across the road in rear or in front of the next tank to be disposed of.

(*c*) Detail BARs, riflemen and bombers to kill motor cyclists, infantry and crews that attempt to dismount.

(*d*) Detail bombers to finish off tanks that are damaged.

(*e*) Use the BAR group to ensure all-round defence and give mutual support to neighbouring squad posts of the platoon position (*of which all road-blocks posts must be part*).

(*f*) After an attack has been beaten off, the squad and A-tk weapon detachment should move to their alternate position as the enemy will probably attempt to neutralize the post by bombardment before attacking again.

(*g*) Register the spot where tanks are to be fired at from all positions.

LAYOUT OF A ROADBLOCK

— IN A TOWN —

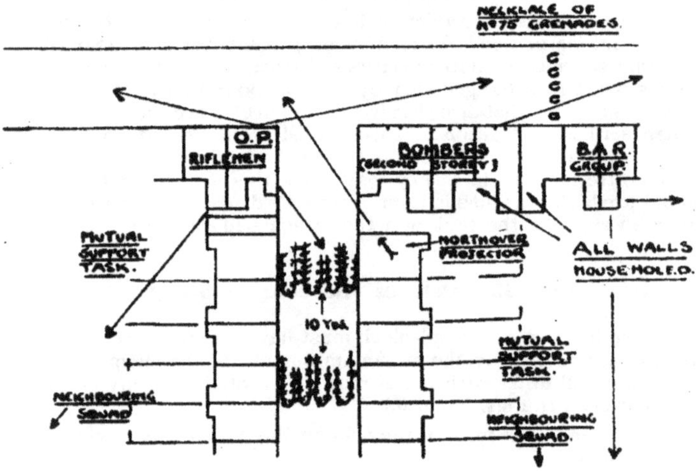

POINTS TO NOTE :—

1. THE BLOCK IS SITED TO PREVENT THE PASSAGE OF ENEMY A.F.V.s INTO THE DEFENDED LOCALITY. SIMILAR BLOCKS WILL BE SITED ON ALL OTHER ROADS LEADING INTO THE LOCALITY.

2. THE SQUAD IS SITED FOR ALL-ROUND DEFENCE.

3. THE POST IS CONCENTRATED.

4. THE BOMBERS HAVE MOBILITY.

FIG. 5.

2. Road-blocks in streets. The same principles apply to road-blocks across streets. The buildings may limit or prevent the use of some types of A-tk sub-artillery. This will be compensated for by the cover given to bombers in the building facing the road-block. Place your bombers above or below the range of tank guns. A-tk rifles can deal with light tanks and can be sited high or low. (*See* Appendix D for use of 3-inch OSB guns.)

Sec. 23. Siting of road-blocks.

1. Road-blocks must be sited to form part of the defences of the locality. Some of the road-blocks constructed in 1940 are not in the right position for present day defence schemes which have been planned to use weapons issued to the Home Guard since the road-blocks were built.

Some of them do not conform to tactical essentials :—

(*a*) They cannot be covered by an A-tk weapon.

(*b*) They are not susceptible to all-round defence.

(*c*) They are not invisible to the attacking tank until he is within range of the A-tk weapon.

If this is the case the block should not be used, or used as a dummy if this fits in with the tactical plan.

2. Screens. All road-blocks, real or dummy, should be screened with blankets or hessian hung across the road high enough to block the view from a tank through periscope or turret top. The tank must then stop to reconnoitre or rush the block which will stop him long enough for the post to destroy him.

3. Pill-boxes. Many road-blocks are protected by pill-boxes constructed at the same time as road-blocks. They should only be used now if :—

(*a*) They can be completely concealed.

(*b*) They are fire-proof against anything but heavy tank gun fire.

(*c*) The loopholes give complete and all-round fields of fire.

Even then they do not make for aggressive defence so can only form part of the squad defences. Communication from inside to those outside is difficult so that control is lost. Weigh carefully their advantages and disadvantages before you keep them in the defence plan. Don't man them just because they are there.

Sec. 24. Opening and closing of road-blocks.

1. The order for closing road-blocks normally will be given by the District or Sub-District Headquarters. If, however, enemy tanks

are approaching a locality, road-blocks may be closed by order of the road-block commander.

Road-blocks must not be constructed which will interfere with the free movement of Field Force units. No road-block must be closed if this will cause delay, except when the enemy are near, and then only upon orders from the local commander.

2. In order to facilitate the opening and closing of Ministry of War Transport road-blocks, the following steps should be taken NOW :—

(*a*) Ensure that the necessary stores are available for closing the block.

(*b*) See that socket covers on the road are easily removable and that the sockets are not obstructed.

(*c*) See that a drill is worked out for closing each type of block so that each man knows what he has to do. To facilitate this, iron rails, etc., should be numbered and methodically stored. Don't forget to maintain all-round protection while the block is being closed.

(*d*) By constant practice, both by day and night, ensure that the block can be opened and closed quickly.

3. **Checking traffic.**

(*a*) Home Guard manning a road-block may be ordered to check traffic and persons using the road. In order not to delay essential traffic on main routes, checking should not normally be carried out unless ordered by higher authority.

(*b*) The following drill will make for efficiency and despatch in passing traffic through the block :—

(i) At a check point it will be necessary to ensure that all traffic is stopped and that no vehicle can rush the block. The road therefore must be partially obstructed. Dannert wire, laid as in FSPB, Part I, Pamphlet 7, 1943, will afford an easy and quickly removable block.

(ii) Men checking traffic will work in pairs. One will check the identity of the occupants of vehicles whilst the other covers them from a concealed position. The sentry doing the checking will carry his arms so as not to impede him in his duties.

(iii) The BAR group will cover the block to deal with emergencies and will find guards or escorts for persons detained. A squad can thus find two pairs of checkers. Squad commanders will not have any special duty other than supervision.

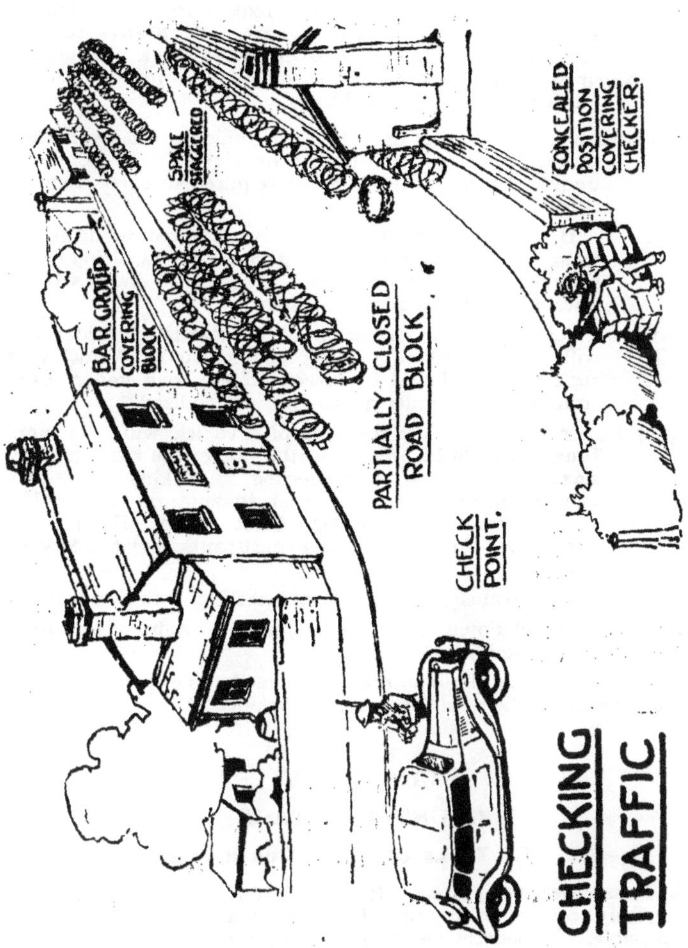
CHECKING
TRAFFIC
B.A.R. GROUP
COVERING
BLOCK
SPACE
STAGGERED
PARTIALLY CLOSED
ROAD BLOCK
CHECK
POINT.
CONCEALED
POSITION
COVERING
CHECKER.

FIG. 6.

(iv) *Method of halting cars.* By day cars will be halted by ordinary police signals; by night a red lamp will be swung horizontally. The signals must always be perfectly clear and the man covering the block will not fire unless the occupants of the vehicle attempt to rush the block or interfere with the sentry.

(v) All persons, whether on foot, or in vehicles, will be checked unless orders to the contrary are given. *NB.*—Children under 16 years of age are not required to carry identity cards.

If possible persons will not be required to dismount from vehicles, and only where grounds for suspicion exist, should vehicles be searched. All cases of doubt will be referred to the squad commander.

(vi) Suspicious persons, or those unable to establish their identity, will be escorted to platoon headquarters. Vehicles of such persons should be placed off the road under cover from air view, under guard and immobilized.

(vii) If, for any reason the checking of a vehicle will take some time, it should be ordered to the side of the road to allow succeeding vehicles to be checked. Checking of the first vehicle should be handed over to another man in the squad—usually one of the BAR group. During the hand-over the vehicle and occupants must be kept covered.

(viii) Extra men must be detailed for checking trams and buses.

Remember, Field Force convoys must be given right of way once their identity is established.

Check-points may be manned for considerable periods. Man management, ie reliefs, will therefore be important.

CHAPTER V.

COUNTER-ATTACK.

Sec. 25. Tasks of Home Guard reserves.

1. In the defended area. It must be the object of the defence not merely to repel an attack but to destroy as many of the enemy as possible. If penetration is made between two localities, the defending garrisons must not only attempt to block further advance (which is merely to react to the enemy) but must exploit their superior knowledge of the ground to cut through and encircle as many of the attackers as possible. Good use of cover will enable the attackers to change direction and their forward elements will be difficult to locate; but attack from a flank will afford the best opportunity of hitting the enemy hard, thus reducing the momentum of his attack, and of isolating and destroying him.

The primary task will not be to provide the final defence against deep penetration. This force must be used in a mobile role, treating localities as strong bases for aggressive action. The main tasks, therefore, will be :—

(*a*) To cut off and destroy enemy penetration. On some occasions the enemy may be enticed forward, with this object in view.

(*b*) To restore a locality that has been overrun, by destroying the enemy in it.

It is most important to provide a mobile reserve, with the primary object of forming a striking force. This reserve may also have to hold a locality eventually. It should, therefore, have prepared the positions which it may later be ordered to hold, but will not normally hold a locality initially because there might be undue delay in concentrating the force from its positions, owing to the difficulty of centralized control, more especially in built-up areas.

It will often be best to provide two mobile reserves, each with a locality allotted as a secondary role. According to the direction of the attack, one will occupy its allotted locality, whilst the other remains available as the striking force ; it is, however, essential that the commander should make the decision on the respective roles sufficiently early to allow of the timely occupation of the locality which is to be defended.

2. In a defended locality.

(*a*) Each battle platoon, company and battalion has its reserve. The defence plan must detail the duties of each reserve, so that the smaller reserves are not squandered on jobs too big for them to tackle. All likely situations should be envisaged and counter-attack by the appropriate reserve practised on the ground during training. Platoon and company commanders must remember that however well the reserves know the ground, it takes time to launch a counter-attack. Therefore, early and accurate information must be passed back to the force reserve commander if the counter-attack is to be put in before the enemy have time to consolidate.

(*b*) *Counter-attack by fire.* An attack can often be halted or broken up by a sudden volume of fire from a flank. This form of counter-attack can be used before the enemy has penetrated the locality. The positions from which the surprise fire will be brought must be reconnoitred and the covered approach to it mapped out. LMGs and automatics are the ideal weapons. The position, however, must not be so far outside the defences as to make it difficult to withdraw the LMG for use in the main defence. The position must not mask flanking fire that can be given from a neighbouring locality to repel the attack.

(*c*) *The counter-attack company or battalion reserve.* Where the enemy has penetrated a vital part of the defences of the locality, he must be dislodged by organized counter-attack usually delivered from a flank. All available fire with all weapons, including sub-artillery, must be brought to bear from neighbouring posts still intact. To be effective this means constant liaison between adjacent squad and platoon posts and with the headquarters organizing the counter-attack. When the position has been reinstated, as much of the reserve as can be spared will be drawn back into the reserve position. Casualties and men from the reserve who have had to be left in the defence posts should be replaced from sub-units not threatened by enemy attack, if the progress of the battle permits.

(*d*) *Platoon counter-attack in towns.* Dislodging enemy penetration in towns will necessitate clearing them out of buildings. The drills given in Secs. 27–29 give a basis for training. They can be adapted to the buildings in any given town and to the weapons with which the sub-unit is armed. Any adaptations must be kept simple. Remember casualties will always upset complicated drills.

(*e*) *Fighting patrols.* From the reserves must be found small active patrols to dominate no man's land and to deal with small groups of infantry or tanks that have infiltrated between localities. Darkness will favour the attacker, who must, therefore, be continuously harassed by night, by stealth, and ambush.

It is, in fact, largely upon energetic and effective patrolling and sniping, both by day and by night, that the successful conduct of the defence depends.

The fighting value of a defence garrison increases in proportion to the activity of its patrolling, which to a large extent deprives the attacker of the initiative, and enables effective defence to be maintained over a larger area. To allow the enemy to obtain superiority, either in patrolling or in close-range sniping, is to court disaster.

CHAPTER VI.

DRILLS FOR TOWN FIGHTING.

Sec. 26. General.

This chapter may be regarded as a continuation of Home Guard Instruction No. 51, Part III—Patrolling. It gives more detailed drills (including a parade ground type) for advanced training for sub-units which will fight in towns. These drills are to assist commanders who find battle drills a help in training. *There is no necessity to use them if they do not fit into the operational and training requirements of units.*

Sec. 27. Parade ground drill for battle platoon advancing to contact and clearing a street.

1. It is essential that all ranks undertaking an operation of this nature should be thoroughly trained, and capable of carrying out instinctively all battlecraft that is required of them in any situation. Home Guard Instruction No. 51, Parts I, II and III should be thoroughly understood, particularly the detailed drill for clearing individual houses.

Fighting in a built-up area is a hard and strenuous job which calls for all the energy and knowledge that a trained man is capable of putting forward. Situations arise suddenly and unexpectedly and must be met firmly and with determination. Certain underlying principles must be thoroughly understood, and are set forth here for the benefit of those Home Guard who have a town fighting role.

2. Principles.

(*a*) Contain the enemy as far as possible before clearing. Enemy who are allowed to move from place to place in any area at will may exact high casualties on the force engaged in their destruction.

During a clearing operation, in the centre of a town, it will rarely be possible to move a seal to the far end of the street which is to be cleared, as this would have to advance through back gardens possibly held by the enemy, and no force large enough to do this with any chance of success could really be spared for the task.

(*b*) Divide the street where necessary into bounds, so that clearing groups are not given an unnecessarily long and fatiguing task. Casualties are to be expected and allowance must be made for re-organization at each bound.

(*c*) Always keep a small reserve in hand to meet any unforeseen emergency such as an unexpected enemy strongpoint.

(*d*) Adopt the drill as laid down for individual squads clearing houses. (*See* Home Guard Instruction No. 51, Part III, Sec. 23.)

(*e*) Obey the principle of fire and movement between clearing groups and BAR groups.

(*f*) Wherever possible, use the street for killing ground and the back gardens for manœuvre.

(*g*) Organize a system of signals whereby control may be maintained throughout by the platoon commander, ie, so that he can follow the progress of each clearing group.

(*h*) Do not hold up the progress of one clearing group to the end of its bound because the other has been held up by the enemy.

(*j*) On locating the enemy in strength, commit your reserve quickly, supporting its attack by EY rifle and any attached sub-artillery. In the event of failure, contain the enemy, learn all you can about his dispositions and weapons, and report to the company commander.

3. **General notes.**

(*a*) *Parade ground.* Any flat ground, minimum size 100 yards square. Mark out with tape or whitening your street and houses as shown in Fig. 7. Where a path already exists, this may be used to represent the street.

(*b*) Three houses only need be marked on either side of the street. Once the drill has been mastered, mark out houses in detail and combine this drill with the drill for a squad clearing a house as laid down in Home Guard Instruction No. 51, Part III, Sec. 23.

(*c*) The layout as shown in Fig. 7 does not provide for an intermediate bound. This can be done, however, by leaving a space to represent a side street and marking out additional houses beyond.

— LAYOUT FOR BATTLE PLATOON ADVANCING TO CONTACT AND CLEARING A STREET —

LAYOUT OF PARADE GROUND — 100x SQUARE —

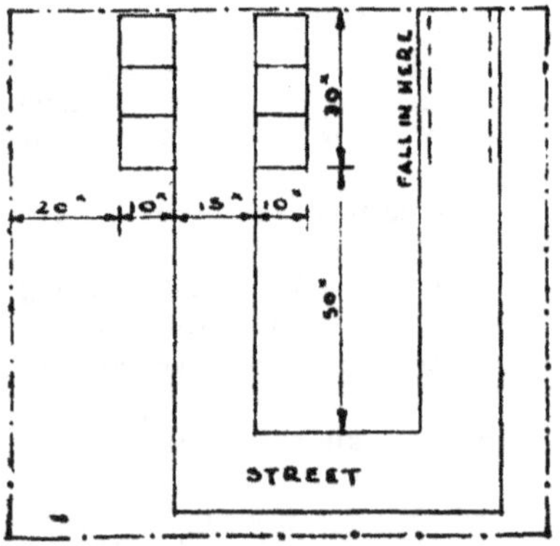

NOTE:- THE STREET IS MARKED OUT THUS ONLY TO FACILITATE CONTROL BY THE INSTRUCTOR AND TO SAVE SPACE. IT MUST BE CONSIDERED STRAIGHT.

FIG. 7.

(*d*) *Drill movements.*

(i) Carried out in quick time at first and at the double when the principles are understood. Keep step.

(ii) In a town weapons will be carried in the ready position, held in both hands.

(iii) Shotguns will be handled like rifles.

(iv) Sten guns will be carried in the ready position.

(*e*) Both clearing groups and BAR groups will act simultaneously. Thus one instructor can control and supervise the whole platoon.

(*f*) This drill combines street clearing with the approach march, or advance to contact, which is considered an essential part of the operation.

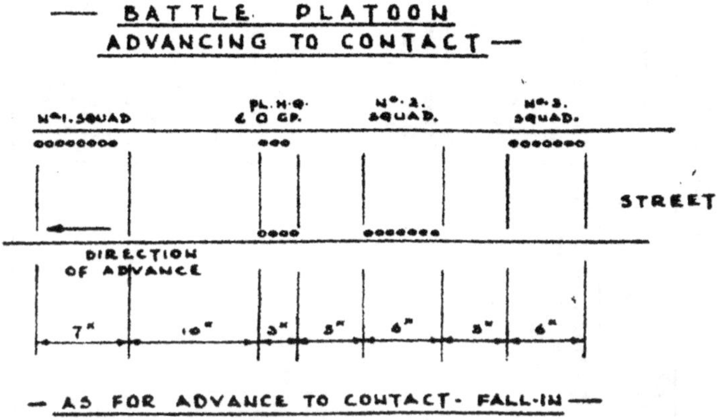

FIG. 8. (*See page 40.*)

PARADE GROUND DRILL FOR BATTLE PLATOON ADVANCING TO CONTACT AND CLEARING A STREET.

Serial No.	Word of command given by	Word of command.	Detail—action by the platoon.	Remarks—what the movement represents.
1	Instructor.	Platoon, as for advance to contact fall in.	The platoon will fall in, closed up, in single file and facing the direction of advance, in the following order (*see* Fig. 8) :— No. 1 (Scout) squad. One yard distance between men. Right hand side: No. 1 rifleman, No. 2 rifleman, Squad commander, No. 1 bomber, No. 2 bomber, No. 1 BAR, 2nd in command, No. 2 BAR —gap of 10 yards— Platoon sniper. Platoon runner. Platoon serjeant. Platoon commander. No. 2 Squad comd. No. 3 Squad comd. Pl rifle-bomber. (Platoon headquarters and "O" group one yard distance between men.) —gap of 5 yards—	There should be marks prepared on the ground where No. 1 rifleman of the scout squad, Platoon sniper, Platoon runner, 2nd in command No. 2 Squad and 2nd in command No. 3 Squad should stand. The distance between these marks are as follows :— No. 1 rifleman Scout Squad. O ↑ 17 yards. ↓ Platoon sniper and platoon runner. O O ↑ 8 yards. ↓ 2nd in command No. 2 Squad. O O ↑ 11 yards. ↓ 2nd in command No. 3 Squad. O

1 *contd.*			2nd in command. No. 1 BAR No. 2 BAR No. 1 rifleman No. 2 rifleman No. 1 bomber No. 2 bomber } No. 2 Squad one yard distance between men. Left hand side. —gap of 5 yards— No. 3 Squad one yard distance between men. Right hand side. { 2nd in command No. 1 BAR No. 2 BAR No. 1 rifleman No. 2 rifleman No. 1 bomber No. 2 bomber	No. 1 Squad commander, platoon commander, platoon serjeant, 2nds' in command Nos. 2 and 3 squads take their parties to the required spots—order arms and stand at ease. In order to save time, the platoon falls in in the order in which it is to move off to make contact with the enemy. It is slightly closed up to facilitate numbering and control by the Instructor. Should the scout squad be on the left of the street then all parties are reversed.
2	Platoon commander.†	As for advance to contact—number.	The platoon numbers from front to rear, each man coming to attention, calling out his number and duty for house clearing, and standing at ease.	This represents each squad checking up that they are present. A very necessary action, at night, in fog or mist or if under enemy shellfire. †Platoon commander comes to attention to give this order and then stands at ease.
3	Instructor.	Platoon commander—lead on.	Platoon commander comes to attention. The platoon remains at ease.	This represents the platoon commander receiving order and acknowledging receipt of it.

Serial No.	Word of command given by	Word of command.	Detail—action by the platoon.	Remarks—what the movement represents.
4	Platoon commander.	Platoon—Observe.	Each man in each squad comes to attention, faces his sector of responsibility, and stands at ease.	The drill is the same for each squad as in squad movement (Home Guard Instruction No. 51, Part III, Diagram 6). Platoon commander's runner and platoon commander look to their front. No. 3 Squad commander looks to his rear. Platoon sniper and platoon serjeant look to their front. No. 2 Squad commander half right and platoon rifle-bomber looks to his rear. The position of the BAR groups in the rear squads does not alter the sectors of responsibility for observation.
5	Platoon commander.	Prepare to advance.	Everybody comes to attention, faces their front and stands at ease.	This implies that although they are facing their front, during all movement they are watching their various sectors. This can be done by cautious movement.

6	Platoon commander.	Platoon will advance —No. 1 Squad leading.	No. 1 Squad commander comes to attention, shouts—Squad advance. No. 1 Squad steps off, rifles at the ready position, opening out to their correct intervals. Platoon headquarters and the remaining two squads follow on at their correct distance in rear, acting on the command of their respective commanders.	This represents the Platoon commander's orders for the advance and the action taken on receipt of them. Correct intervals are :— Scout Squad—5 yards between men. 10 yards between groups. 30 yards between squads and platoon headquarters. 1 yard between men in platoon headquarters and Nos. 2 and 3 Squads.

—End of Phase 1—

7	Instructor (As the leading man of the scout squad reaches the first marked building.)	Platoon under fire.	Everybody halts—moves two yards off street—stands at ease. No. 1 Squad only shouts DOWN — CRAWL — OBSERVE—SIGHTS.	This represents the whole platoon taking cover off the street, the scout squad crawling into a position from where they can engage the enemy. The fire may come from only one sniper. Clearing must, however, commence from here, as even one enemy left behind can cause many casualties.
8	No. 1 Squad commander.	Enemy 100 — Red house on left—fire as targets appear.	Squad comes to attention, then stands at ease.	This represents the scout squad returning the fire of the enemy at intervals when they see a target. The rifle group may take up positions for all-round defence.

Serial No.	Word of command given by	Word of command.	Detail—action by the platoon.	Remarks—what the movement represents.
9	Seconds in command Nos. 2 and 3 Squads.	Squad—Scouts forward—move.	Squads come to attention. Nos. 1 and 2 riflemen move to the head of the squads which advance to a point 15 yards away from the street on their respective sides and 70 yards in rear of the first marked building. On reaching their positions the 2nds in command call—Squad halt. Whereupon the squads halt and stand at ease.	This represents the automatic move forward of the squads to an assembly position in rear of platoon headquarters. This position will generally be in the back gardens. The move to this position may be covered by scouts, and will generally be made through the back gardens.
10	Seconds in command Nos. 2 and 3 Squads.	Squad — all-round protection — BAR group right, rifle group left—move.†	Squads come to attention. Each man moves to his correct position in arrow-head, and turns to face his sector. Squads stand at ease.	This represents all-round protection at assembly positions. †The BAR and rifle groups are interchangeable and go either right or left of the leader.
			—End of Phase 2—	
11	Platoon commander.	Runner—follow me.	Platoon commander and runner come to attention and move off to the right of No. 1 Squad commander, keeping two yards off the street.	The platoon commander with his runner only move forward and observe. It is essential to contact No. 1 Squad commander and learn from him all information about the enemy. The platoon commander and his runner will generally move up through the back gardens. This is represented by their moving two yards off the street.

12	Platoon commander.	No. 1 Squad—you are fire squad.	Squad commander only comes to attention.	The platoon commander appreciates that No. 1 Squad cannot themselves clear the street, but are able to cover the killing ground from their present position. He therefore makes them fire squad.
13	Platoon commander.	Reconnaissance.	Platoon commander (only) comes to attention.	This represents the platoon commander's reconnaissance from a point of vantage.
14	Platoon commander.	" O " group and platoon headquarters.	" O " group and platoon headquarters come to attention and move up their respective sides of the street, keeping two yards away from the street, until No. 3 Squad commander is on the right of the platoon commander, and No. 2 Squad commander with platoon headquarters is in a position two yards off the street and abreast of the platoon commander. They halt and stand at ease.	This represents the " O " group and platoon headquarters moving up near to platoon commander by a covered route (represented by the two yards off the street) and taking up a position of observation inside a building from where they can hear the platoon commander's orders.
15	Platoon commander.	Enemy in this street. We will clear the street from here. Usual method. No. 1 Squad fire squad, cover street.	(i) " O " group disperses. (ii) Nos. 2 and 3 Squad commanders move outwards 15 yards and call out—No. 2 (or No. 3) Squad. The squads come to attention	The platoon commander decides to clear the street by using squads on their own sides, to avoid crossing the street. The platoon serjeant, rifle-bomber and sniper are on the

Serial No.	Word of command given by	Word of command.	Detail—action by the platoon.	Remarks—what the movement represents.
15		No. 3 Squad right of street. No. 2 Squad left of street. First bound—there. Platoon headquarters present position. Signals, white handkerchief from ground floor of each house cleared, success signal from first floor of end house. I shall be—here. Study the ground. Any questions—move.	and move up to their commanders, who halt them as they arrive. (iii) Platoon headquarters remains where it is.	left of the street and can thus add to the fire on to the killing ground. No. 2 Squad commander is already on his own side of the street. No. 1 squad has the dual role of covering the street and being prepared to act as reserve if necessary. Should the street be long or tortuous, it will be necessary to introduce bounds. In this case the first bound is indicated in the platoon commander's orders. In order to indicate the limit of the next bound the platoon commander points out to No. 3 squad commander the feature on the left of the street opposite which he is to stop, and describes this feature to No. 2 squad commander, who will not be able to see it until he reaches it.
16	Squad commanders :— All Squads— No. 1 Squad.	Enemy in this street. Platoon is going to clear from here—end	On the word " Any questions " each man will come to attention, ask any question or say	The squad commander's orders differ from the platoon commander's in several respects.

16 *contd.*		of bound there. Usual method. No. 3 Squad right— No. 2 Squad left. We are fire squad and will kill anyone entering this street. BAR group there. Rifle group there. Signals, white handkerchief from ground floor of each house cleared. Success signal from first floor. Platoon headquarters — there. Study the ground. Any questions— move.	"No, corporal," and stand at ease.	(i) Platoon commander's method becomes squad commanders information own troops. (ii) Certain details, eg point of entry and position of BAR group, must be contained in the squad commander's orders. Squads will now be re-organized as for house clearing, ie into clearing group and BAR group. (*See* Home Guard Instruction No. 51, Part III, Sec. 23.)
	Nos. 2 and 3 Squads (at the same time).	Enemy in this street. Platoon is going to clear street. No. 1 Squad — fire squad. No. 3 Squad right of street (No. 2 Squad left of street). We will clear left (right) of street. Usual method. First bound—there. BAR group—there. Point of entry—that door.	Squad commanders point out position for BAR group, and point of entry for clearing group.	

Serial No.	Word of command given by	Word of command.	Detail—action by the platoon.	Remarks—what the movement represents.
16 *contd.*		Signals, white handkerchief from ground floor of each house cleared. Success signal from first floor. Platoon HQ there. Study the ground. Any questions—BAR group move.	On the words " Any questions" each man comes to attention, asks any question or says " No, Corporal " and stands at ease.	
17	Seconds in command Nos. 2 and 3 Squads.	BAR group—follow me.	Seconds in command lead BAR groups, together with No. 2 rifleman to positions indicated —10 yards outwards from clearing groups.	This represents BAR groups moving off to their flanks to give covering fire on to points of entry of clearing groups, also on to back gardens, windows, etc., in the vicinity.
18	Seconds in command Nos. 2 and 3 Squads.	BAR group—halt.	BAR groups halt in the required positions and stand at ease facing their appointed tasks.	
19	Seconds in command Nos. 2 and 3 Squads.	BAR group—observation normal—fire as targets appear.	BAR groups come to attention, then stand at ease.	This denotes that they are in the position to give covering fire as required.
20	Squad commanders Nos. 2 and 3 Squads.	Doormen.	No. 1 rifleman and No. 2 bomber of both squads come to attention and move off to their point of entry. (*See* Home Guard Instruction No. 51, Part III, Sec. 25, Drill Serial 5.)	Squad commanders, having ascertained that their BAR groups are in position, commence clearing.

21 or 21A	Instructor.	Enemy. No enemy.	*See* Home Guard Instruction No. 51, Part III, Sec. 25, Drill Serial 6 or 6A.	
22	Squad commanders Nos. 2 and 3 Squads.	Advance.	*See* Home Guard Instruction No. 51, Part III, Sec. 25, Drill Serial 7.	
23	Squad commanders Nos. 2 and 3 Squads.	Doormen.	*See* Home Guard Instruction No. 51, Part III, Sec. 25, Drill Serial 8.	
24	Instructor.	House cleared.	Squad commanders move to street side of house and wave handkerchief, then return to centre of clearing group and stand at ease. Platoon commander, platoon serjeant, No. 1 Squad commander all come to attention and then stand at ease.	To shorten the drill, the detail for clearing individual houses is not practised during the early stages of this drill. This represents the understanding of the signal from the clearing group that the first houses have been cleared.
25	Instructor.	Mousehole.	Squad commanders come to attention and call out—Mousehole there. Doormen (No. 1 rifleman and No. 1 bomber) move to point indicated and stand facing the wall one yard apart. Both come to attention and then stand at ease.	This represents either mouseholing through the wall to the next house, or forcing an entry through the roof.

Serial No.	Word of command given by	Word of command.	Detail—action by the platoon.	Remarks—what the movement represents.
or 25A		Outside.	Squad commanders come to attention and call out—Doormen, next house. The doormen (No. 1 rifleman and No. 1 bomber) move out of house to back of next house, take up normal positions at point of entry chosen. Squad commanders move to back of houses, watching doormen. No. 2 bomber remains in the house until the next house has been cleared. He stands at ease.	This represents the alternative method of entering the next house, should it be impossible to mousehole. No. 2 bomber is left to counter the possibility of enemy mouse-holing through from the house which is being cleared.
26 or 26A	Instructor.	Enemy. No enemy.	*See* Home Guard Instruction No. 51, Part III, Sec. 25, Serial 6 or 6A.	
27 to 29	As in Serial Nos.	22 to 24 above.	As soon as the houses are cleared, ie Instructor—House cleared, squad commanders call their No. 2 bombers into the house. They enter and stand at ease.	
30	Instructor.	Clearing groups — your BAR groups cannot cover your next entry.	Squad commanders Nos. 2 and 3 Squads come to attention.	This represents the squad commanders' own appreciation of this fact.

31	Nos. 2 and 3 Squad commanders.	Clearing group — observation normal — fire as targets appear. BAR group—there.	Clearing groups come to attention, then stand at ease. Seconds in command come to attention.	This represents the clearing groups ready to give covering fire for the BAR groups as they move.
32	Seconds in command Nos. 2 and Squads.	BAR group—follow me.	Seconds in command lead BAR groups to positions indicated—10 yards outwards from their clearing groups.	This represents BAR groups moving up to a position from where they can cover the entry into the next house.
33	Seconds in command Nos. 2 and Squads.	BAR groups—halt.	BAR groups halt in the required positions and stand at ease facing their appointed tasks.	
34	Seconds in command Nos. 2 and Squads.	BAR group—observation normal—fire as targets appear.	BAR groups come to attention, then stand at ease.	This denotes that the BAR groups are in a position and ready to give covering fire.
35 or 35A	As in Serial Nos.	25 or 25A above.		
36 and 37	As in Serial Nos.	22 and 23 above.		
38	Instructor.	Bound clear.	Squad commanders move to side of house nearest the street and wave handkerchief. Shout —Success signal. Platoon	This represents squad commanders signalling from upper floor, indicating that their task is completed.

Serial No.	Word of command given by	Word of command.	Detail—action by the platoon.	Remarks—what the movement represents.
38 *contd.*			commander, platoon serjeant, No. 1 Squad commander come attention, then stand at ease.	Represents understanding of signals.
39	Platoon commander.	We will advance to first bound—move.	Platoon serjeant and No. 1 Squad commander come to attention.	This represents the platoon commander's orders for the advance up to the end of the first bound.
40	Platoon serjeant.	Platoon HQ—follow me.	Platoon HQ is led round the back of the houses on the left to No. 2 Squad's position, they enter the house.	This represents the move up, under cover, of the platoon HQ and No. 1 Squad. On certain occasions this movement will have to be done in the street. It will be appreciated that a fair measure of covering fire is available.
	No. 1 Squad commander (at the same time).	No. 1 Squad—follow me.	No. 1 Squad is led round the back of the houses on the right to No. 3 Squad's position, they enter the house.	
	Platoon commander (at the same time).	Runner—follow me.	Platoon commander and the runner move round in rear of No. 1 Squad.	
41	Platoon serjeant.	Platoon HQ—halt.	Platoon HQ takes up positions as shown in Fig. 9, halts and stands at ease.	
	No. 1 Squad commander (at the same time).	No. 1 Squad—halt.	No. 1 Squad takes up positions as shown in Fig. 9, halts and stands at ease. The platoon commander and runner halt at position as shown in Fig. 9 and stand at ease.	

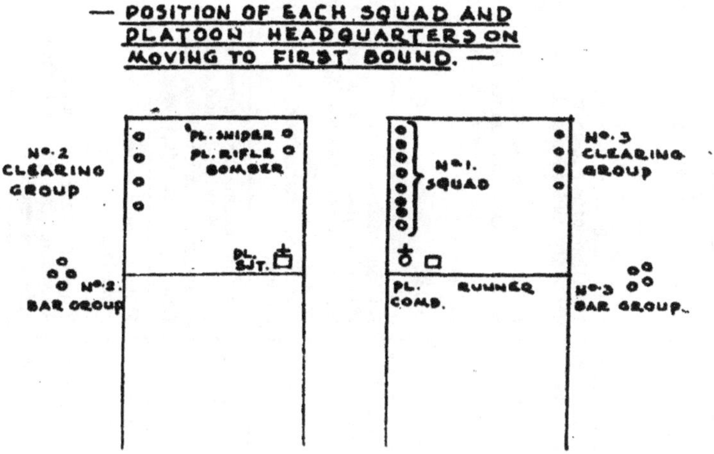
— POSITION OF EACH SQUAD AND PLATOON HEADQUARTERS ON MOVING TO FIRST BOUND. —
No. 2 CLEARING GROUP
PL. SNIPER
PL. RIFLE BOMBER
PL. SJT.
No. 2 BAR GROUP
No. 1 SQUAD
No. 3 CLEARING GROUP
PL. COMD.
RUNNER
No. 3 BAR GROUP

NOT TO SCALE

FIG 9.

Serial No.	Word of command given by	Word of command.	Detail—Action by the platoon.	Remarks—what the movement represents.
42	All Squad commanders.	Squad as for advance to contact—number. (At the same time).	Each man in turn comes to attention, calls out his number and duty and stands at ease.	This represents the reorganization either at the end of the first bound or at the close of the operation.
	Platoon commander.	Pl HQ as for advance to contact—number.	Pl HQ numbers in the same way. Each man states the number of unexpended rounds he has left.	
43	Platoon commander.	" O " group and platoon serjeant.	All Squad commanders and Platoon serjeant come to attention, and report in turn, No. 1 (or 2 or 3) Squad. Casualties, ammunition, information.	The Platoon commander knows the casualties, ammunition expenditure and information of Pl HQ because he called the roll himself.
44	Instructor.	Platoon commander—report.	Platoon commander comes to attention, shouts—Bound clear—casualties, ammunition, information. Stands at ease.	
45	Instructor.	Continue to clear.	Platoon commander comes to attention.	
46	Platoon commander.	We will clear to next bound—there. No. 1 Squad, fire	Squad commanders remain at attention, and give out their orders, as before.	

46. *cont.*		squad—cover street. No. 3 Squad, right of street. No. 2 Squad, left of street. Pl HQ — present position. Signals as usual. I shall be here. Study the ground. Any questions.		
47	Instructor.	Platoon—steady.	Platoon stands at ease.	Instructor criticizes the drill.

— PLATOON BATTLE DRILL FOR CLEARING TWO ROWS OF OCCUPIED HOUSES — ALTERNATIVE METHODS —

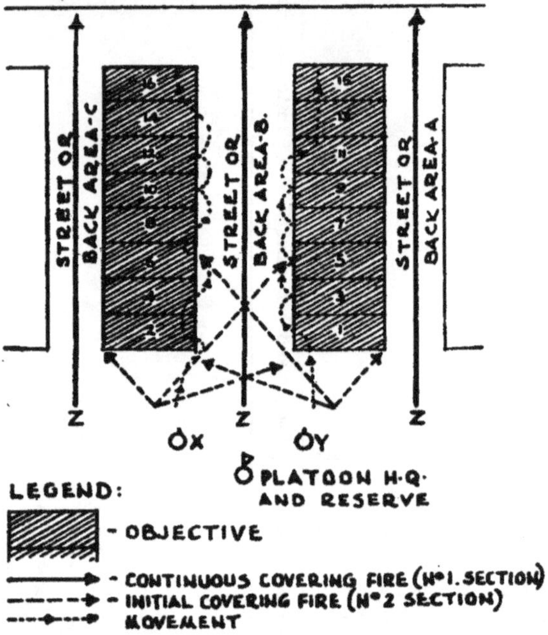

FIG. 10.

NOTES.

1. X represents No. 2 Squad with clearing group ready to assault and covering group giving initial covering fire.

2. Y represents No. 3 Squad disposed similarly to No. 2 Squad.

3. No. 1 Squad (Z) gives covering fire, possibly assisted by part of Platoon headquarters.

4. Platoon headquarters and reserve follow either No. 2 or No. 3 Squad.

Alternative methods.

The two leading squads can advance up the *backs* of the two rows of houses (ie via entrances in A and C), when B would be the killing area. Alternatively, one row at a time may be taken on, when B might be the killing area, with the two leading squads leap frogging through the houses and back gardens between A and B or C and B.

To approach by back ways is often the best method of gaining access to houses ; and this method, where circumstances are suitable, also allows the concentration of a large volume of covering fire on the killing ground. A disadvantage is that the fire of the leading squads will be less effective for covering each other.

4. **Alternative methods.** Under certain circumstances (for instance, where there are no back gardens or the ground behind the houses is unsuitable for advance, or where smoke is available to cover the attack) the drill should be adapted to make the street the approach and the rear of the building the killing ground. (*See* Fig. 10 and film No. B/C 433—" House to House Fighting.")

Sec. 28. Platoon battle drill for clearing a house.

1. This drill is based upon the principles of fire and movement. It is designed to enable a platoon commander to co-ordinate an attack upon a house by two squads simultaneously, supported by an organized fire plan.

Like all battle drills it must be employed, and adapted if necessary, with common sense.

Don't let the fire plan become rigid. The commander must control the weapons under his command to give the maximum fire support without delaying or endangering the clearing groups.

2. The problem in clearing a strongly defended house will always be to get to the top. Once this has been attained the subsequent clearing of rooms will be done by squads using the drill given in Home Guard Instruction No. 51, Part III.

3. The platoon will be organized as a battle platoon and should have the support of a Northover or 3-inch OSB gun detachment to afford added covering fire. Squads will be organized into BAR and clearing groups as for clearing a house.

The rifle bomber and sniper of platoon headquarters will be used to thicken-up the covering fire on to the entry side of the house.

Likely preparations by the enemy to strengthen their defences have been given in the sections on preparing a house for defence in Appendix A.

4. **BAR groups.** Two BAR groups will be employed to cover the killing grounds and destroy any enemy who attempt to escape.

The third BAR group will be employed to give covering fire to the clearing groups and to destroy any enemy showing himself in the house ; its fire will be controlled by the platoon commander. If the platoon has only two squads, one BAR group must be detailed for this task.

5. Clearing.

(*a*) The platoon commander will order two clearing groups into the house. He will give a dividing line, eg stairs, as inclusive to one or other group.

The object of both groups will be to reach the top of the house as quickly as possible.

Phase I. Each clearing group will select a point of entry. One BAR group, reserve clearing group, platoon sniper and rifle-bomber, a Northover or 3-inch OSB gun detachment if available, will give covering fire on to ground and first floor windows. If necessary the 3-inch OSB gun firing from a flank will be able to blow a suitable mousehole as a point of entry for one or both clearing groups. The (3-inch OSB) gun can also be employed from a flank to deal with any enemy firing through loopholes. Sub-artillery fire must be carefully controlled by the platoon commander.

Each clearing group will use the drill given in Home Guard Instruction No. 51, Part III, to effect an entry. Phase I is completed when both clearing groups have entered. (*See* Fig. 11.)

Phase II. No. 2 bomber of each clearing group will wait downstairs and watch platoon headquarters. Remainder of each clearing group will try to reach the first floor either by ceiling-holing or by the stairs. Groups must keep to their own side of the dividing line as ordered by the platoon commander.

Covering fire will lift to second floor windows on completion of Phase I.

Phase II ends when one or other clearing group reaches the first floor.

Phase III. Whichever clearing group first reaches the first floor will give a success signal to platoon headquarters.

Platoon headquarters will then order the unsuccessful clearing group by signal to disengage and reinforce success. If this is NOT possible No. 3 (reserve) clearing group will be used to reinforce success. The unsuccessful group will come into reserve as soon as it can disengage.

Two groups will thus have reached the first floor and each will endeavour to gain the second floor.

PLATOON BATTLE DRILL FOR CLEARING A HOUSE.

PHASE - I.

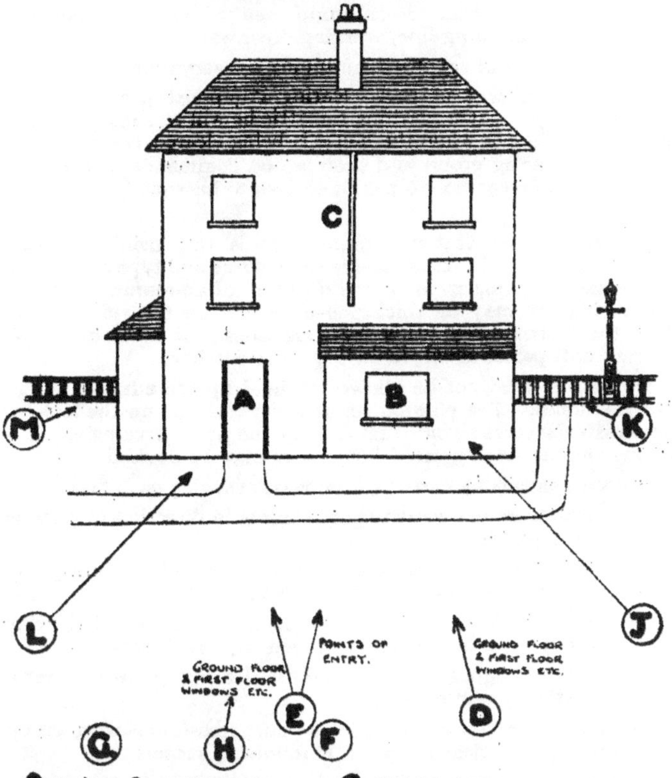

A — LEFT POINT OF ENTRY.
B — RIGHT POINT OF ENTRY.
C — DIVIDING LINE.
D — Nº3 SQUAD B.A.R. GROUP.
E — RIFLE-BOMBER.
F — PLATOON COMMANDER.
G — Nº3 SQUAD CLEARING GROUP.
H — ATTACHED SUB ARTILLERY.
J — Nº1 SQUAD CLEARING GROUP.
K — Nº1 SQUAD B.A.R. GROUP.
L — Nº2 SQUAD CLEARING GROUP.
M — Nº2 SQUAD B.A.R. GROUP.

FIG. 11.

Covering fire will lift to the third floor on receipt of the success signal.

Phase IV. The previous phase is repeated until both groups have reached the attic. Each group then will clear the rooms on its side of the dividing line, working downwards.

Covering fire will consist of sniping by observation.

(*b*) No. 2 bomber of each clearing group must keep one floor behind his group. On reaching the attic he will rejoin his group and guard the top floor while the house is being cleared. He is the link between his clearing group and the platoon commander; therefore he must be within earshot to pass messages to his squad.

6. Control. The platoon commander is responsible for controlling the attack. He must decide the volume and type of covering fire necessary, bearing in mind the question of ammunition supply. The covering fire may be thickened-up either by the rifle-bomber and/or the Northover firing No. 36 grenades; or the 3-inch OSB gun firing anti-personnel shells through the windows.

Covering fire must not be allowed to hold up the advance to the top of the house. The platoon commander must be on the lookout for successive success signals and control the fire accordingly. The following signals are suggested but others may be devised :—

(*a*) Success signals by clearing groups on reaching each floor :—

Handkerchief waved from window in direction of platoon headquarters.

(*b*) Signal by platoon commander to unsuccessful clearing group that the other clearing group has succeeded :—

Right or left hand out pointing to the successful clearing group, or a handkerchief waved in that direction.

On this signal the unsuccessful clearing group will automatically reinforce success.

(*c*) Signal by platoon commander to unsuccessful clearing group that reserve clearing group is following success :—

As in (*b*) above, with flag held straight up in other hand also.

(*d*) Final success signal that the house is cleared :—

Any appropriate signal, which must be acknowledged by platoon headquarters and all BAR groups before anyone leaves the house.

NOTE.—Verey lights, if available, are alternatives for all the above.

PLATOON BATTLE DRILL FOR CLEARING A HOUSE.

PHASE - 2.

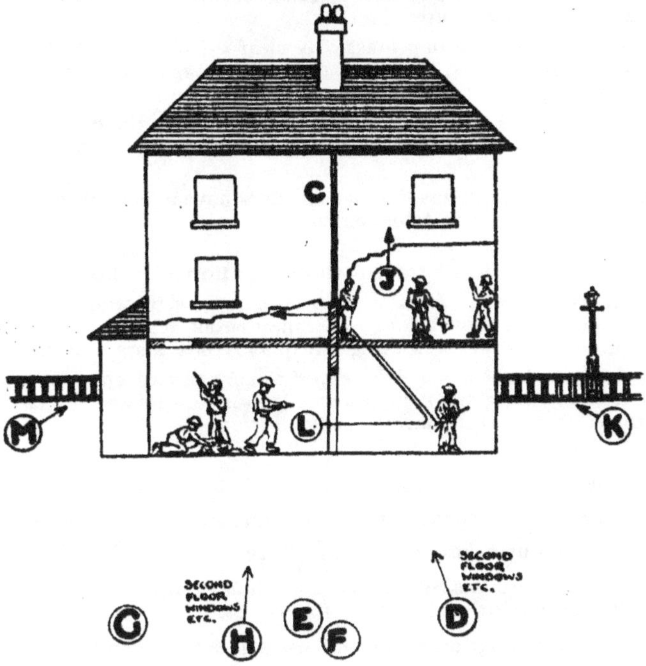

LEGEND AS FOR PHASE - I

POINTS TO NOTE :-

1. SUCCESSFUL CLEARING GROUP (J) SIGNAL TO PLATOON COMMANDER — HE ACKNOWLEDGES

2. UNSUCCESSFUL CLEARING GROUP (L) MOVE THROUGH (J) TO OWN SIDE OF HOUSE.

FIG. 12.

7. **Special points.**

(*a*) The first aim is to reach the top of the house. The platoon commander must control the covering fire as so not to endanger successful clearing groups.

(*b*) Each clearing group must only clear sufficient on any floor to enable them to reach the next one and to signal success to the platoon commander.

(*c*) If the third clearing group is passed through, the unsuccessful one will come into reserve and be prepared to reinforce in the next phase.

(*d*) All clearing groups must at all times have a lookout on watch for signals from the platoon commander.

Sec. 29. Drill for hasty occupation of a house.

1. **Introduction.** It may often be necessary to occupy a house to oppose enemy infiltration. This may entail fighting to get there and protection while it is being put quickly into a state of defence.

This operation can be more expeditiously carried out if a squad has trained, using the drill below. It can be adjusted for use by platoons if the task requires a larger force.

2. **The Drill.**

1. Commander appreciates situation and issues warning order.

2. BAR group takes up covering position.

3. Clearing group searches necessary houses, using drill in Home Guard Instruction No. 51, Part III, Sec. 23.

4. Clearing group takes up fire positions for all-round defence.

5. Commander makes reconnaissance and gives orders for final fire positions, which will include posting snipers and/or observers.

6. The working party will consist of every one except No. 1 on BAR, snipers and/or observers. They will prepare their fire positions.

7. Carry out defence work in priority given in Appendix A.

Note.—An alarm signal will be arranged when all work stops and fire positions are occupied.

3. **Withdrawal.** When ordered to withdraw, groups will thin out and move back to pre-arranged rendezvous, always observing the principle of fire and movement.

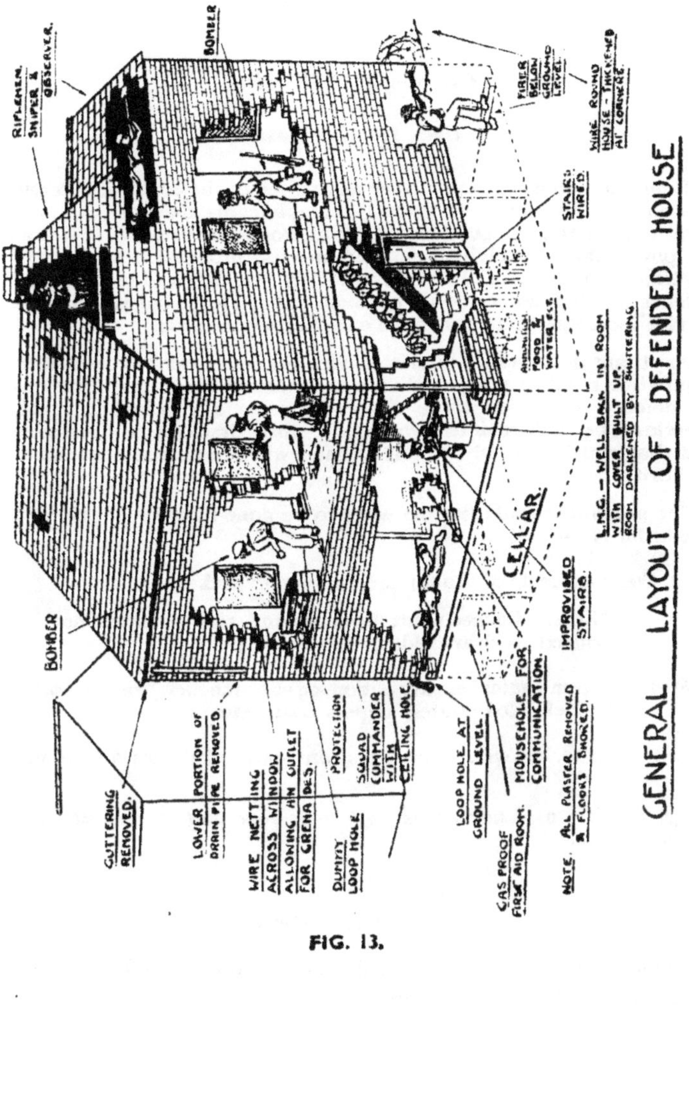
RIFLEMEN, SNIPER & OBSERVER.
BOMBER
FIRER BELOW GROUND LEVEL.
WIRE ROUND HOUSE - THICKENED AT CORNERS.
STAIRS WIRED.
AMMUNITION FOOD & WATER ETC.
L.M.G. - WELL BACK IN ROOM WITH COVER BUILT UP. ROOM DARKENED BY SHUTTERING
CELLAR.
IMPROVISED STAIRS.
MOUSEHOLE FOR COMMUNICATION.
BOMBER
GUTTERING REMOVED.
LOWER PORTION OF DRAIN PIPE REMOVED.
WIRE NETTING ACROSS WINDOW ALLOWING AN OUTLET FOR GRENADES.
DUMMY LOOP HOLE
PROTECTION
SQUAD COMMANDER WITH CEILING HOLE
LOOP HOLE AT GROUND LEVEL.
GAS PROOF FIRST AID ROOM.
NOTE. ALL PLASTER REMOVED & FLOORS SHORED.
GENERAL LAYOUT OF DEFENDED HOUSE

FIG. 13.

APPENDIX A.

DEFENCE WORKS.

Sec. 1. General.

Every commander should have a schedule of the construction and demolition that must be done to complete his defences. It will form part of the defended locality War Book (*see* Sec. 19). Just as a Home Guard is a civilian engaged on vital production for most of his time prior to "ACTION STATIONS," so, much of the essential defence construction can only be taken in hand after our intelligence service indicates that invasion is once more imminent.

Anything that unduly interferes with the war work of the civilian population must be postponed until the moment when considerations of defence outweigh those of production. The schedule must, therefore, be divided into two parts; work that can be done now and that which can only be put in hand when authorised by higher authority.

The schedule should list the work to be done in order of priority. The order is :—

(*a*) Clearing fields of fire for each killing ground.

NOTE.—Concealment from ground and air must not be sacrificed to clear fields of fire and view.

(*b*) Protection against enemy action, eg slit trenches, weapon pits, OPs, defended houses, snipers posts, etc.

(*c*) Obstacles, eg wire, minefields, anti-tank obstacles and road-blocks.

Fig. 13 *gives a picture of the work to be done putting a house in a state of defence.*

Sec. 2. Penetration.

Defences are worthless unless bullet-proof against small arms fire. Check them with this protection table :—

Protection Table.

Safe thickness in inches against armour-piercing LMG fire up to 7·92 millimetres (burst of 20 rounds) or splinters from a 100 lb. HE bomb bursting not less than 30 feet away.

Serial No.	Material.	Safe thickness in inches.	Remarks
1.	Earth or loam as in parapets	60	
2.	Chalk as in parapets	60	Variable.
3.	Clay as in parapets	72	Variable.
4.	Sand, loose or between boards	30	
5.	Brick rubble confined between boards ..	18	
6.	Coal between boards..	24	
7.	Road metal (1½ in.–2 in.) between boards	14	
8.	Sandbags filled with :—		
	(*a*) Rubble	30	
	(*b*) Earth	30	
	(*c*) Road metal	20	
	(*d*) Shingle	20	
	(*e*) Sand	30	
9.	Brickwork in lime mortar	18	
10.	Concrete, unreinforced	12	
11.	Mild steel plate	1¼	
12.	Timber	60	Variable.

Observation at the weekly demonstration of penetrations at the GHQ Home Guard Town Fighting Wing show that :—

(*a*) Three short bursts from Sten *will* penetrate a lightly barricaded door, barricade consisting of a mattress and a chest of drawers filled with plaster.

(*b*) A sloping slate roof is penetrated by one round (·303) fired from a rifle.

(*c*) A chimney stack composed of 4½-inch brickwork is penetrated by six well aimed shots.

(*d*) One No. 69 Grenade will generally blow in or breach a lightly barricaded door, and will remove at least one brick from a 4½-inch wall.

(*e*) The Sten will *not* generally penetrate stretcher sandbags or a 4½-inch wall. This is due to the fact that shots rarely strike the same spot twice in quick succession.

(*f*) Two well aimed shots (·303) from a rifle will generally penetrate even dry stretcher sandbags, also a 4½-inch wall. One shot will generally do the latter, if the wall runs at 90 degrees to the line of fire.

(*g*) Six well aimed shots (·303) from a rifle will generally penetrate a 9-inch wall.

(*h*) Four well aimed shots (·303) from a rifle will generally penetrate header sandbags.

(*j*) A long burst fired from a Lewis (·300) will generally penetrate a 9-inch wall. A short burst will penetrate stretcher sandbags.

Sec. 3. Design of protective works.

When constructing field-works or putting buildings in a state of defence, remember that the maximum heights over which weapons can be fired are :—

(*a*) Rifle or LMG—lying	9–12 ins.
(*b*) Rifle or LMG—sitting	2 ft.
(*c*) Rifle or LMG—kneeling	3 ft.
(*d*) Rifle or LMG—standing	4 ft. 6 ins.
(*e*) 2-pr	2 ft.
(*f*) Smith gun	21 ins. { sights are 1 ft. above barrel.
(*g*) Northover Projector—	
From tripod at lowest	2 ft. 1 in.
From tripod at highest	2 ft. 10 ins

Reduce by 4½ inches on soft ground where spades will dig in.

Sec. 4. Field-Works.

FSPB, Part I, Pamphlet No. 7, 1943, now in preparation, will be given a wide distribution to Home Guard sub-units. It contains nearly all the information required by Home Guard for the construction of field-works.

Sec. 5. Defence of buildings.

1. Home Guard defence will, in a great many cases, employ buildings for a variety of purposes. Therefore some additional notes on this subject are given below :—

(*a*) *Construction work.* This must be carried out in the order given in Sec. 1 of this Appendix.

(*b*) *Fields of fire.* Arrange necessary demolition in conjunction with Civil Defence authorities, and RE if available.

(*c*) *General considerations.*

(i) *Tactical requirements.*—The first consideration is that a house or building must satisfy the tactical requirements, which may be to provide a firm base from which the mobile elements of the garrison can operate, to withstand assault, to cover an obstacle, to support another building, to provide a link in a chain of communication, or to deny a particular approach.

(ii) *Durability*.—A very large number of bombs or shells are required to affect seriously a built-up area. The most durable buildings are those with steel or reinforced concrete frames; the next are those of stone construction. Brick buildings are weak unless shored up, while wooden buildings, once they have become a target, may be death traps. The effect of fire upon a building should be considered and all non-essential inflammable material removed.

(iii) *Surroundings*.—Adequate fields of fire are, of course, essential in order that tactical offensive requirements may be met, but buildings must also be considered from the point of view of their own defence. A house may be rejected, even if half the area round it is flat and open, if the other half has approaches that are difficult to guard and therefore the more likely to be used by the enemy.

A house selected for defence should be inconspicuous—an advantage inherent in one of a row of houses—and should not be open to observation from a dominating feature.

Approaches to and from a building should be available out of view of the enemy.

Full use should be made of weapon slits sited at the edges of gardens. Such positions may be readily concealed from the air and are not liable to be buried if the buildings collapse. Moreover, the beaten zone of LMGs sited at ground level is greater than when fired from the upper floors of a house. Alternative positions in the house should, however, be selected even if weapon slits can be sited outside.

(iv) *Defensive capabilities*.—Buildings, including their interiors and the roofs, must be capable of all-round defence. Their size and design, combined with the surroundings, will serve as a guide to the minimum strengths of garrisons.

(v) There must be no distinction of place or person when a building is required for defensive purposes.

2. Reconnaissance of a building. Points to look for are :—

(*a*) Observation posts.

(*b*) Fields of fire. Primarily these will be required to enable the garrison to carry out its main tasks. The actual defence of the building itself is a secondary consideration.

(*c*) Extent to which loopholes are required.

(*d*) Strength of building, and whether walls are bullet-proof.

(*e*) Entrances and exits. Too many will be a source of weakness, and will necessitate additional material and labour for blocking them up.

(*f*) Communications with adjacent houses, and with fire posts in the garden and outhouses, if any.

(*g*) Alternative positions.

(*h*) Facilities for defence against bombing and artillery fire.

(*j*) Water supply : for drinking and for putting out fires.

(*k*) Material and resources available in the building and in adjacent buildings.

(*l*) Rough estimate of work and material required for putting building into state of defence.

(*m*) Dressing station.

(*n*) Cookhouse.

(*o*) Latrines.

3. **Local protection.** This should be considered for both the outside and inside of a building, and with the different conditions of day and night in mind.

Outside a building—by day, and sometimes by night, one or two positions outside a building may afford better protection than inside and may prevent the enemy getting near enough to neutralize the defences in the building itself.

4. **Windows and loopholes.** Sufficient windows and loopholes are required for alternative positions, but the number of loopholes should be kept as low as possible because they weaken the structure of the building and involve labour and material. Loopholes, especially those for observation, should be made in unexpected places such as under a window-sill or through the tiles of a roof.

The following considerations should be borne in mind :—

(*a*) To obtain a wide arc, loopholes are often made in the form of rectangular slits. They are, however, more effective if shaped like a V with the wider section on the inside. Since they are also likely to be used for firing at targets above and below, they should be roughly cone-shaped to present as small an exterior aperture as possible.

(*b*) The edges of a loophole, especially when made in brickwork, will be liable to splinter when hit by a bullet. If possible, a protective lining, eg sacking, held in place by wire netting, should be installed to reduce splinter effect. For the same reason sandbags nearest to the firer or observer should be filled with earth or sand, and not shingle or stones.

(*c*) When not in use a loophole or window requires some form of cover, bullet-proof if possible, that can be placed in position to prevent the enemy seeing or firing through it.

(*d*) Methods of concealment and deception include making dummy loopholes indistinguishable from the real ones; painting or draping well-known and likely objects against or round loopholes; use of lace curtains; and placing of dummy figures at apertures not in use.

(*e*) When using a window, a firer should normally have a kneeling or standing position prepared on either side of the window and protected by the wall. As he often will require to fire downwards, these positions should be raised well above the level of the sill upon a chest of drawers filled with rubble and sufficiently far away to prevent his rifle protruding through the window. A lying position does not always allow sufficient freedom for firing at widely varying angles, especially in elevation.

(*f*) Some loopholes should be made inside the building in case the enemy break in.

(*g*) Wire netting or similar material over windows and loopholes, especially those near ground level, serves to keep out hand-thrown grenades. The wire should hang or be fastened below the outside sill to prevent any missile lodging on the sill. A small gap or over-lapping slip should be made to allow grenades to be thrown out or a firer to lean out if necessary.

(*h*) Care should be taken to prevent smoke by day, and artificial light by night, being seen through a loophole or window from the outside. A screen should be provided between the head of the man at the loophole or window and the source of light.

(*j*) Loopholes at ground level, eg when using the grating from a cellar, should have a small shelving trench dug below them on the outside. The object is to catch grenades that roll towards the base of the wall or drop after hitting the wall above and to cause them to explode below the level of the loophole.

(*k*) It may be necessary, in order to give adequate protection, for some of the ground-floor windows not required for defence purposes to be blocked up and made bullet-proof. Boards with earth or shingle between them will be effective. The practice, however, may indicate to the enemy that a given house is occupied.

(*l*) Observation in all directions must be arranged. A loophole covered with appropriately painted wire gauze from the meat safe permits an observer to see without being seen.

(*m*) Remove all glass. Strew it on likely approaches. It crunches under foot and gives notice of anyone approaching. Block up unwanted windows (curtains give cover from view).

SHORING-UP A BUILDING.

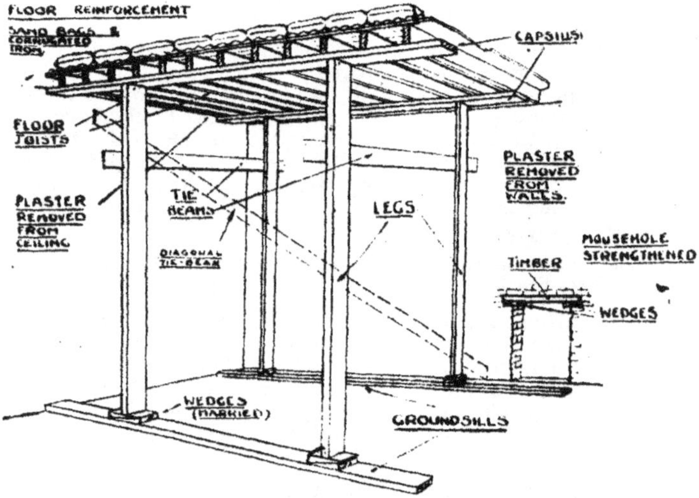

DETAIL OF SHORING

FIG. 14.

Sec. 6. Reinforcement of the building.

1. **Introduction.** The construction of loopholes and mouseholes between rooms will to some extent have weakened the building.

The weaker the building the more these works must be strengthened (necessarily adding additional weight) to make the walls bullet-proof opposite weapon positions.

Therefore, the next thing to do is to decide how much reinforcement is required.

2. Shoring-up a building. (*See* Fig. 14.)

Shore-up ceilings where a building is not made of steel and concrete. Shoring must start from the bottom based on a concrete or stone floor. Where this does not exist take joists from neighbouring or damaged houses and place them horizontally on a solid foundation. Hold cap-sills against the upper floor joists at right angles to them. Adjust the ground-sills to come vertically under cap-sills. Insert legs between the two. Secure in place by wedges.

That is: take two narrow wood wedges and tap them in from opposite directions between the ground-sill and each leg.

Nail the tie beams to legs as in Fig. 14. Diagonal tie beams, as shown in dotted lines, will strengthen structure if head room and field of fire permit.

3. Reinforcing upper floors. A floor may often have to be made bullet-proof by laying down sandbags. In this case it usually requires strengthening.

Place corrugated iron on floor boards to distribute the weight. Lay sandbags close and hammer out to avoid cracks.

If sandbags are not available pile plaster and brick rubble on the corrugated iron and cover with old flooring or doors.

4. Reinforcing a mousehole. The bad effects on a wall caused by a mousehole can be to some extent remedied by :—

Squaring off top of mousehole.

Making small recesses by pulling out bricks on either side at the top :—

Cut timber of corresponding length. Insert in recesses.

Force up to take the weight with wedges. (*See* Fig. 14.)

5. Additional points. Fix boards with nails points upwards on window-sills. Deny staircases to the enemy by nailing boards lengthways over the treads.

If necessary leave one plank width for normal use. Keep plank handy to nail in place in an emergency.

If a hole is made in each ceiling, the enemy can be observed and bombed from the upper rooms. The hole can be used for ordinary movement (have an improvised ladder) instead of the stair, which can then be obstructed with wire as well as the boards.

Mouseholes made from room to room and house to house for intercommunication should be concealed by cupboards or furniture.

Remove drain pipes, creepers, etc., for at least ten feet from the ground.

Note.—Remember to do this to neighbouring undefended houses or it will give away your position.

Be ready to fight fires. Collect available buckets and stirrup pumps.

Keep all available receptacles full of water. Make emergency sanitary arrangements.

Sec. 7. Outside the defended house.

1. **Slit trenches and weapon pits** should be dug as alternative positions. They should not be sited to help the enemy in an attack if unoccupied, but should be far enough from building to be clear of falling masonry.

2. **Wire.** Immediately around the house, wire should be fixed as inconspicuously as possible and securely staked. It will hamper the enemy if he tries to use the walls of the defended house as cover.

In alleyways and small courts which are blind spots, trip wires with tins attached should be *suspended shin high* to give warning of enemy approach.

Trip wires should be used for the same purpose on roofs and tops of walls leading to the squad post.

In towns many of the routes leading to the defended position must be kept open for patrols and runners. Where permanent wiring cannot therefore be done, knife rests must be made and kept handy.

Sec. 8. Booby traps.

1. Passive obstructions can be greatly strengthened by the use of simple booby traps. They make the progress of the enemy slower and have a considerable moral effect. They must be intelligently sited not to interfere with our own patrols and always be well concealed.

The methods of setting them should be ingenious and varied so that the enemy does not learn easily how to detect them.

The principles :—

(*a*) *Preservation of outward appearances.* If time permits, cover up all traces such as wire and spoil.

(*b*) *Constricted localities.* Choose a close site when setting traps, avoid a bottle-neck when expecting them.

(*c*) *Double bluff.* This is the principle of laying a well-concealed trap close to a fairly obvious one. This tends to attract the attention to the obvious one, and, in avoiding it, the well-concealed trap is set off.

(*d*) *Inconvenience.* The employment of obstacles and things which might be removed by troops entering the building.

(*e*) *Curiosity.* The principle of using booby traps in connection with souvenirs, crooked pictures, food and drink containers, etc. Never be curious. Do not touch anything unnecessarily.

(*f*) *Everyday operation.* Traps operated by opening or closing doors or windows, telephones, light switches, WC plugs.

2. The following improvised booby traps can be easily set by the

Home Guard, who should observe the principles laid down regarding their siting :—

(*a*) *The* 36 *grenade.* This is set up in conjunction with a trip wire. The wire is permanently fixed at one end, and attached to a 36 grenade with pin removed, inserted in a cocoa tin at the other. The cocoa tin is nailed to a fixed board.

As the wire is tripped the 36 grenade is pulled out of the tin thereby releasing the lever. *See* Fig. 15.

—SETTING A BOOBY-TRAP WITH A 36 GRENADE—

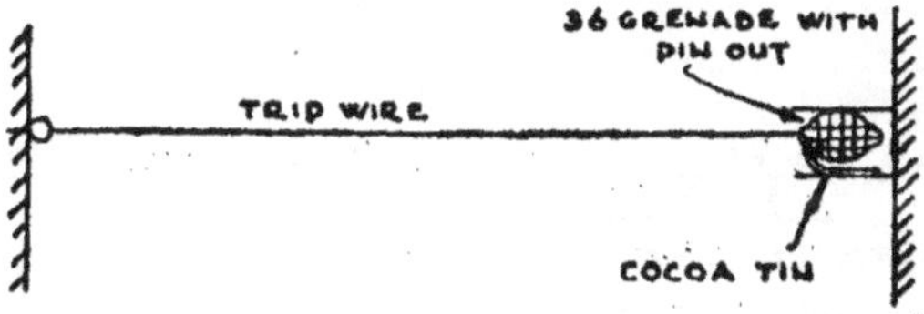

FIG. 15.

(*b*) *The* 69 *or* 73 *grenade.* Set up in connection with the opening of a door. The tape is partially unwound. The lead weight is fastened to the lintel of the door and the grenade supported either on the door top, or on a small ledge constructed. As the door is opened it comes in contact with a stop placed on the floor. The grenade is jarred from the door or ledge. The pin is removed by the tape. Grenade burst on hitting floor. *See* Fig. 16.

—SETTING A BOOBY-TRAP WITH 69 OR 73 GRENADE—

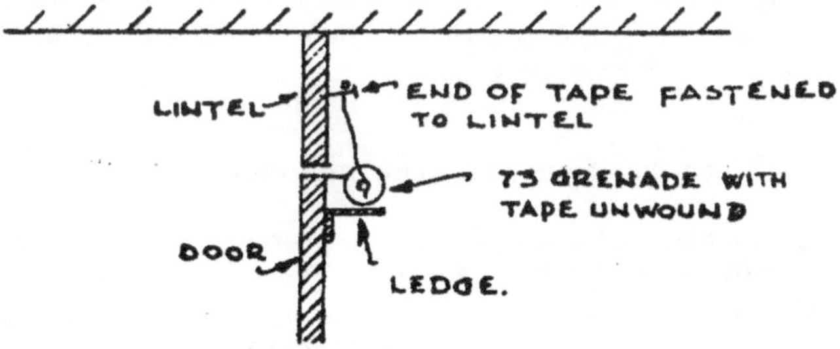

FIG. 16.

(*c*) *Electrically exploded improvised booby trap.* This depends on the following for its effect :—

(i) A charge exploded by a low tension electric detonator.

(ii) A simple electrical circuit completed by the coming together of two contacts.

At Fig. 17 is shown a simple trip-wire trap using a clothes peg and wedge. The jaws of the clothes peg are made into electrical contacts by nailing on pieces of tin.

—SETTING AN ELECTRICALLY EXPLODED BOOBY TRAP—

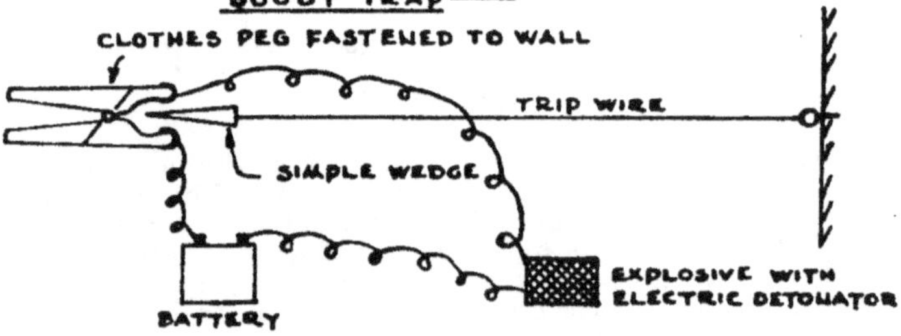

FIG. 17.

(*d*) Many other similar devices can be improvised by pieces of tin and wire, such as a trap set in a drawer with pieces of tin as contacts.

Sec. 9. 2-pr. anti-tank gun emplacement.

Fig. 18 and the notes give the measurements and method of construction of a 2-pr. A-tk gun emplacement.

The exact shape and depth will depend on the shape of the ground and the traverse required. The wheels or extra ammunition can be placed in the sides of the pit, or in a separate emplacement.

— 2-PR. ANTI-TANK GUN EMPLACEMENT —

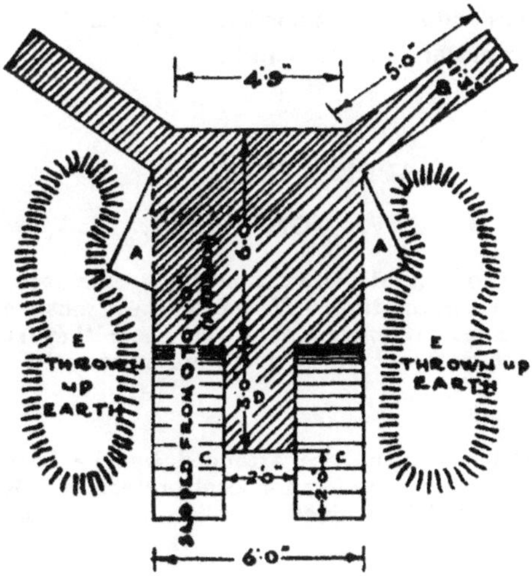

FIG. 18.

NOTES.—

A. Portions cut away to allow traverse if side shields are fitted.

B. Slits for front legs.

C. Ramps for running gun in and out.

D. Slit for trail leg.

E. Spoil forming parapet.

To construct the emplacement :—

(*a*) Dig the main pit and ramps.

(*b*) Push in the gun and site it exactly.

(*c*) Open the legs and mark out portions A, B and D.

(*d*) Pull the gun out and dig A, B and D.

APPENDIX B.

OBSERVATION POSTS.

1. **Object.** The object of observation posts, like reconnoitring patrols, is to gain information. Therefore they must not fight except in self-defence. If enemy approach them they should lie doggo and continue to report unless given orders to retire.

2. **Organization.**

(*a*) Observation posts should be arranged by the battalion or company intelligence officer, unless for local protection only of sub-units. Personnel should be trained observers who also know how to report.

(*b*) The size of an observation post will depend upon its location and the length of time it is likely to be manned. It should not consist of less than three men. If permanently manned it must consist of not less than one NCO and six men. No man must be made to observe continuously for a period of more than two hours. Observers must be doubled at night.

3. **Orders.** Orders to an observation post must include :—

(*a*) Area of responsibility.

(*b*) How and when to report.

(*c*) How long they will remain in observation and details of reliefs if any.

(*d*) Administration arrangements regarding food, etc.

Observation posts must have detailed knowledge of the defensive layout and of all patrols which are being sent out.

4. **Equipment.** Each observation post must be equipped with the following :—

(*a*) Map or panorama sketch of the country under observation, correctly orientated.

Points of the compass will be marked around this map or sketch so that the bearing of any point can be read straight off (*see* Elementary Map Reading, **1941**).

In cases where the exact location of an occurrence cannot be given the bearing will be given with an approximate distance from the observation post.

(*b*) Field glasses or telescope (if possible).

(*c*) Periscope (in towns.)

(*d*) Situation report forms. These will be filled in with the information obtained and forwarded to headquarters when called for.

(*e*) Suitable communications. Alternative methods must be provided. Line, visual, wireless or carrier pigeons are all suitable. Orderlies, if employed, must not betray the position of the observation post by bad battlecraft.

5. **Duties of NCO IC post.** The NCO or man in charge of the post is responsible for organizing reliefs and for ensuring that the post is continually and efficiently manned. All information must be given to each relief coming on duty.

He is responsible that all reports are short, accurate and complete, and rendered when required.

He must ensure that suitable facilities exist for rest, feeding and sanitation for men on the post when not on duty.

An observation post is only effective as long as it remains unobserved and concealed, and as long as it is able to get reports back to headquarters. Success depends upon battlecraft, keen eyesight, methodical and careful observation and quick accurate reports. Only by constant practice can proficiency be maintained. At no time, either during practice or in active operations, allow bad track discipline to give away your observation post.

APPENDIX C.

SENTRIES.

1. Home Guard train only for their operational role. Therefore ceremonial sentries have no place.

2. At night all sentries must be posted in pairs. One sentry will be posted at the odd hour and the other at the even to ensure the maximum degree of alertness.

3. No sentry shall be on duty for more than two hours consecutively.

4. The usual periods are two hours on and four hours off.

5. Men not on duty must be made to rest. Position of reliefs must permit men to be wakened for their tour of duty without disturbance of the rest.

6. It follows that a sentry post manned for any length of time must consist of :—

2 NCOs and 6 men
or
1 NCO and 7 men.

Where there are not two NCOs the seventh man is on the alert in the post to wake the guard commander and the guard if necessary.

7. Sentries must be relieved and posted by an officer or NCO.

8. At a headquarters there will be written orders for the guard and the sentries.

9. Sentries must know :—

(*a*) Their responsibilities.
(*b*) Location of the rest of the guard.
(*c*) Area they must watch.
(*d*) Position of neighbouring sentries.
(*e*) Movements of our patrols or other troops in their area.
(*f*) When to fire.
(*g*) Alarm signals and passwords.
(*h*) Responsibility for gas detectors.
(*j*) Action to be taken with our own troops arriving at the headquarters or post.

10. **Drill for sentries.**

(*a*) (i) They will be posted so that they can warn the post silently.

(ii) The double sentries posted at night will be in touch to be able to communicate with each other without movement or noise.

(iii) Remain concealed as long as possible.

(*b*) Sentries may be divided into three categories :—

(i) *At a headquarters.* The guard will not be turned out except for large parties not readily identified.

When individuals or small parties approach, sentry says just loud enough to be heard :—

"HALT! WHO GOES THERE?"

If the order is obeyed, the man or leader of the party will say "Friend" or say who he is in more detail.

Sentry will say :—

"ADVANCE, ONE, TO BE RECOGNIZED"

The sentry will repeat this order if there is more than one, for each member of the party to advance. If the credentials are in order, the man or party will be passed on to the responsible officer or NCO they wish to see.

If credentials are not in order, the man will be handed over to guard commander.

If persons approaching the guard fail to obey the sentry's order, he will say :—

"HALT OR I FIRE"

If the man or party still does not halt, he will fire.

NOTE.—Before "ACTION STATIONS" the method given in ACI 1228/40 will be used.

(ii) *At a squad post on "active operations."* The main object of a sentry is to prevent the post being rushed by a fighting patrol while the squad is at rest. Therefore the drill must differ from that used at a headquarters. The sentry must be completely silent and unseen.

On suspicion of enemy approach, he will waken the post silently.

The squad will be ready to fire. The person or party will be allowed to approach as near as possible with safety. The sentry will say, just loud enough to be heard :—

"HALT"

If the order is obeyed, the squad commander will order one man to advance.

The squad will cover the man and the rest of the party

If the orders are not obeyed the squad will open fire. Do not challenge too soon.

(iii) *At a road-block.* For duties and drill *see* Chapter IV.

APPENDIX D.

TACTICAL HANDLING OF 3-INCH OSB GUN (SMITH GUN) IN TOWN FIGHTING.

1. Penetrations.

(*a*) The 6-lb anti-tank bomb penetrates 80 mm. of armour plate at 50 yards. It will make a 2 feet diameter hole in a 9-inch reinforced concrete wall and has considerable effect behind it.

(*b*) At 100 to 200 yards the 8-lb anti-personnel shell penetrates a 9-inch brick wall at an angle of 90 degrees. At an angle of 45 degrees or less the hole is usually 3 feet in diameter. It also loosens the brickwork surrounding the hole made so that the size of the hole can easily be increased. Oblique fire is often the only method in towns. It will be noted that this is the most effective use of the 8-lb shell when directed against buildings.

2. **Mobility.** The gun and trailer can be towed behind a 10 hp car. Alternatively, one motor cycle can tow the gun, and one the trailer. It will be manhandled into its final position. (*See* Figs 19 and 20.)

The weight of the gun is 5 cwt. 1 qr. 16 lbs.
The weight of the trailer is 3 cwt. 22 lbs.

The wheel track of gun and trailer is 3 ft. 6 ins. The diameter of the wheel is 4 ft. The size of the wheel and the lightness of the gun permits the crew to manœuvre the gun and trailer (separately) over almost any obstruction and through any passage of the necessary width. For crossing very steep slopes or broken walls, planks, doors or shutters can be used as ramps. If it is desired to get it from one street to another under cover, a few shots will loosen up enough brickwork to make a gap big enough to push the gun through

3. **Angle of fire and crest clearances.** The maximum depression is 7 degrees and elevation 40 degrees. Fire can therefore be brought to bear at almost any point of the face of a defended house in support of an attack. However, the flat trajectory of the shell at ranges under 200 yards necessitates careful watch on crest clearance. To clear a wall 3 ft. high the gun must be sited at least 20 yards in rear; this often means that it must be fired in the open or through a mousehole.

3. **Fire positions.** When fired off a hard surface, eg a road, the gun, if weighted with three sandbags, will jump back about 2 inches and if unweighted about 6 inches. In neither case is the accuracy of the shot affected. Under all circumstances, however, it will be necessary to re-lay the gun after each shot.

3-INCH OSB GUN—MANHANDLING ACROSS ROUGH COUNTRY.

MANHANDLING THE
SMITH GUN
ACROSS ROUGH GROUND.

FIG. 19.

3-INCH OSB GUN—COMING OUT OF ACTION IN THE OPEN USING TOGGLE ROPES

COMING
OUT OF
ACTION IN THE
OPEN — BY USING
TOGGLE ROPES

FIG. 29.

The gun can be fired from any type of ground provided the wheel-base is roughly level. Bricks or rubble will form a perfectly good fire position. Any tendency for the gun to wobble on a hastily occupied position can be satisfactorily overcome by inserting half a brick under the wheel. Any pronounced tilt of the gun platform will tend to make the gun fire low in the direction of the tilt.

The point of burst should not be nearer than 100 yards from our own troops in the open or 50 yards under cover (the shield gives cover to No. 1 only).

5. **Firing through a mousehole.** Bring the gun up to wall at the position located during reconnaissance. Put gun in position and determine size and position of mousehole.

NOTE.—Remember the muzzle of the gun will always be several feet in rear of wall because of the carriage and space required to turn the gun on to its side. The sights are 1 foot above the barrel (measuring from base of barrel to top of sights) so mousehole must be high enough for aiming. If the mousehole is to be made by explosive, withdraw gun to safety first. (*See* Fig. 21.)

6. **Equipment for the use of the gun in towns.**

(*a*) Four toggle ropes per gun detachment.

Use. Passed through the towing eye they are used to pull over rough ground to get gun out of action.

(*b*) A reconnaissance stick (*see* Fig. 22). This consists of wire loop or piece of 1-inch piping fastened on to a stick. The whole should be painted black and white to make it readily visible. This stick can easily be made by units. Its uses are as follows :—

(i) The detachment commander, when reconnoitring a position, can roughly check for crest clearance. For final check look through the barrel when the gun is in position.

(ii) Having selected the gun site, the detachment commander can leave this stick in the ground to mark where the gun is to go.

7. **Drill for tactical handling in a town.**

(*a*) *General duties of detachment.*

(i) *Detachment commander.* Commands the detachment, and is responsible for all orders. He selects the gun site, and controls the fire of his gun. He is responsible that his equipment is kept clean and lubricated, that spare parts are serviceable and interchangeable, that small stores are complete, and that his gun is kept ready for action

3-INCH OSB GUN—IN ACTION THROUGH MOUSEHOLE.

FIG. 21.

(ii) *No.* 1. Operates the breech, lays and fires the gun. In the open, owing to lack of cover, he may also load the gun and set the range.

(iii) *No.* 2. Sets the range and loads the gun when behind cover.

(iv) *No.* 3. Carries ammunition from the trailer to No. 2. He also drives the towing vehicle.

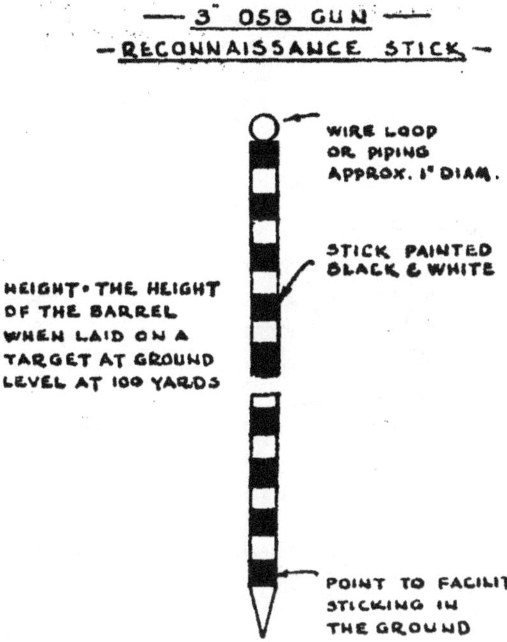

FIG. 22.

NB—The stick must be the height of the barrel and not of the sights which are placed 1 foot above the barrel.

(*b*) *Diagram of gun and detachment positions for manhandling* (see Fig. 23).

(*c*) *General instructions.*

(i) Any flat ground, ideal size 200 yards by 100 yards, to include a street, will do for practice. The street can be marked out with tape if necessary. Walls, if non-existent, should also be represented.

(ii) Enemy house is represented by a flag or swastika, and by the umpire instructor.

(iii) For drill movement *see* Home Guard Instruction No. 51, Part II, Sec. 12 para. 1 iii. The detachment, unless otherwise ordered, will drill with arms slung.

DETACHMENT COMMANDER.	RIGHT OF TOWING EYE
No. 3	LEFT OF TOWING EYE.
No. 1.	AT BASE WHEEL.
No. 2.	AT APEX WHEEL.

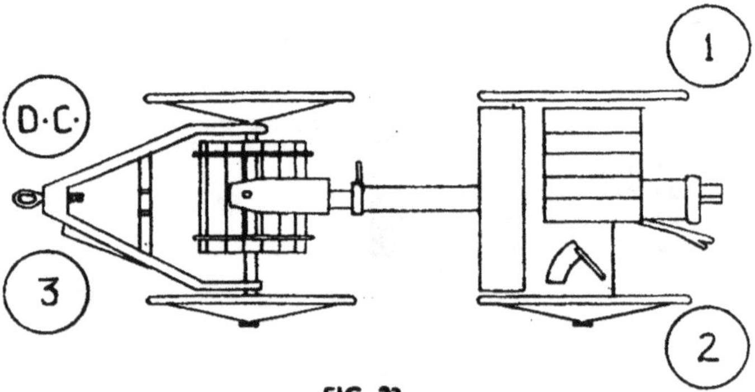

FIG. 23.

NOTE.—The gun wheels are referred to as "base wheel" and "apex wheel." This facilitates explanation and relates to the lower and upper wheels when the gun is overturned for action.

(iv) One BAR group is attached to represent and impress the need for covering fire.

(v) This drill is designed to teach the tactical handling of the Smith gun, without battlecraft.

DRILL FOR TACTICAL HANDLING OF 3-INCH OSB.

Serial No.	Word of command given by	Word of command.	Detail—action by detachment and BAR group.	Remarks—what the movement represents.
1	Instructor.	Detachment and BAR group—number.	The detachment and BAR group are in file, the detachment forming the front rank and the BAR group the rear. They face the gun two paces from it. Each man comes to attention in turn, calls out his number and duty, and stands at ease. The duties are :— *Detachment Commander.* — I command the detachment, am responsible for all orders, select the gun site, and control the fire. *No.* 1.—I fire the gun. I also load and set the range when in the open. *No.* 2.—I assist No. 1 and pass ammunition. I load, and set the range when the gun is firing from behind cover. *No.* 3.—I carry ammunition from the trailer to the gun site. I also drive the towing vehicle. *BA R Group.*—We are attached for covering fire and all-round protection.	The instructor represents the higher commander checking over the detachment and BAR group, and giving order for the operation.

Serial No.	Word of command given by	Word of command.	Detail—action by detachment and BAR group.	Remarks—what the movement represents.
2	Instructor.	Take post.	The detachment and BAR group come to attention and fall in. The detachment takes up positions around the gun (*see* Fig. 23) and stands at ease. The BAR group falls in in single file on the right and in line with the detachment.	This represents the detachment and BAR group falling in, either at their start point, or at the point at which the gun is detached from the towing vehicle.
3	Detachment commander.	Advance.	The detachment and BAR group move off. No. 1 disengages the brake.	Represents the detachment and BAR group advancing to contact.
4	Detachment commander.	Halt—unlimber.	The detachment halts, disconnects the trailer and stands at ease. No. 1 applies the brake. The BAR group automatically takes up positions for all-round observation and stands at ease. Positions are :— BAR group commander looks to his front. No. 1 turns three-quarters right. No. 2 turns three-quarters left.	This represents the arrival of the detachment and BAR group at a point on the road nearest the objective.
5	Detachment commander.	I am going to make a recce — BAR group remain present position — Nos. 2 and 3 trailer there ; prepare ammunition. No. 1	The detachment commander and No. 1 spring to attention and bring weapons to " the ready position." The detachment commander moves forward 15 paces and halts.	Represents detachment commander's recce, No. 1 covering him forward and he in turn covering No. 1 forward.

5 *cont.*		collect two No. 74 grenades and follow me.	No. 1 moves forward 15 paces and halts on the left of the detachment commander, both stand at ease. Nos. 2 and 3 draw trailer to the position indicated by the detachment commander, No. 2 taking up a position on the left and No. 3 on the right of the trailer. They come to attention. BAR group commander gives an anticipatory fire order. BAR group comes to attention then stands at ease.	Represents trailer being drawn into position under cover. Indicates that they are preparing ammunition. Represents the BAR group ready to give fire on to any targets that appear.
6	Detachment commander (at the gun site).	No. 1—prepare grenades. Target—that house. Gun site—there. You will prepare mousehole there, then re-join detachment — await my order. Move.	Detachment commander and No. 1 come to attention and sling arms. The detachment commander moves forward two paces, halts, comes to attention, and places his " Recce stick " on the ground, shouts—Gun site, then turns about and marches five paces, halts and stands at ease. No. 1 moves forward two paces, comes to attention, shouts—" Mousehole," turns about and marches five paces, halts and stands at ease.	Represents detachment commander appreciating situation and No. 1 preparing his No. 74 Grenades. Represents detachment commander going to gun site and placing his " Recce stick " to mark it, he then moves back to a position from where he can give his orders to the remainder of the detachment. Represents No. 1 preparing mousehole and rejoining detachment commander.

Serial No.	Word of command given by	Word of command.	Detail—action by detachment and BAR group.	Remarks—what the movement represents.
7	Detachment commander.	Nos. 2 and 3 and BAR group commander—join me. Enemy house 100. We will come into action at recce stick. BAR group—there, covering fire. Any questions. BAR group—move.	Nos. 2 and 3 and BAR group commander move off to a position two paces from and facing the detachment commander who then turns about. (All are now facing the objective), No. 1 turns about to watch the front. On the word " Any questions," each man will come to attention, ask any question or say " No, corporal," and stand at ease.	The detachment commander gives orders for the advance to the gun site. He arranges for the BAR group to cover movement.
8	BAR Group commander.	BAR group—follow me.	The BAR group comes to attention and is led to the spot indicated.	Represents BAR group moving to a position from where they can cover the advance of the detachment.
9	BAR Group commander.	BAR group—halt.	BAR group halts, turns to face the objective and stands at ease. Shouts—DOWN—CRAWL — OBSERVE — SIGHTS.	On reaching their position the BAR group get into a position ready to fire.
10	BAR Group commander.	Enemy house — 100 —covering fire.	BAR group comes to attention.	Represents fire being opened.

11	Detachment commander.	Detachment — take post—toggle ropes.	The detachment comes to attention and falls in, each man taking up his correct position around the gun and standing at ease. (*See* Serial 2.) The detachment commander and No. 3 place their toggle rope through the towing eye supporting the loop end at their shoulders.	This represents the detachment falling in at the gun, ready to manhandle it across rough ground anticipated by the detachment commander.
12	Detachment commander.	Detachment — advance—double.	The detachment moves off at the double towards the gun site, the detachment commander and No. 3 pulling on the toggle ropes, Nos. 1 and 2 turning each wheel.	This movement is covered by the BAR group.
13	Detachment commander.	Detachment—halt.	The detachment halts and stands at ease.	
14	BAR Group commander.	BAR group—stop—fire as targets appear.	BAR group stands at ease.	
15	Detachment commander (at gun site).	Action—there.	The detachment manœuvre the gun into the position indicated. The detachment commander and No. 3 remove their ropes from the towing eye.	The gun will be turned to the left on reaching the site, thereby ensuring that the base wheel is in the correct position for overturning the gun.

Serial No.	Word of command given by	Word of command.	Detail—action by detachment and BAR group.	Remarks—what the movement represents.
16	Detachment commander.	Brake on—over.	No. 1 applies the brake then stands and pulls on the base wheel, detachment commander lifts the apex wheel, No. 2 assists as necessary. When the gun is in position and roughly level, the detachment form up as follows :— Detachment commander—facing the objective, six paces from the gun in the direction of the street. No. 1 immediately behind the gun. No. 2 one pace to the right of No. 1. No. 3 seven paces in rear of the gun. All stand at ease.	This represents overturning the gun on to its base wheel. The detachment commander moves to a position from where he can observe the fire (through a periscope if necessary). No. 3 journeys between the gun and the trailer. In the open some form of smoke, eg the SIP Grenade, should be used to cover this movement.
17	Detachment commander.	100 — HE House — Right first floor window—4 rounds HE —load.	Nos. 1 and 2 come to the kneeling position. No. 2 sets the range. No. 1 (at the same time) lays the aim. No. 1 opens the breech, looks through the barrel, and reports " Crest clearance."	When in the open, No. 1 will set the range and load the gun. No. 2 will prepare and pass the ammunition carried up by No. 3 from the trailer.

17 *cont.*			No. 2 (at the same time) goes through the motions of preparing the round. No. 1 closes the breech, and reports " ready."	
18	Detachment commander.	Four rounds — Fire.	No. 1 fires and opens the breech —No. 2 re-loads. No. 1 re-lays and fires. The detachment commander remains at attention. The above procedure continues until the required number of rounds have been fired, or the order to stand fast is given.	No. 1 re-loads if the gun site is in the open. This represents observing the fire.
19	Instructor.	Shot—low (or high).	Detachment commander orders " Stand fast "—up 50 (or down 50)—Same target. No. 2 re-adjusts the sights. No. 1 opens breech (at the same time) and reports " Crest clearance." No. 2 re-loads. No. 1 closes the breech and reports " Ready." Detachment commander orders " Go on." Firing continues.	It is essential to check for crest clearance again in this case, as by altering the range the trajectory is also changed.

Serial No.	Word of command given by	Word of command.	Detail—action by detachment and BAR group.	Remarks—what the movement represents.
20	Instructor (during the motions of firing).	Gun won't fire.	No. 1 shouts "Misfire" then re-cocks the firing mechanism and again presses the firing lever.	
or 20A	Ditto.	Gun firing all right	No. 1 carries on firing.	
		or Gun still won't fire.	No. 1 shouts "Second misfire"—pause one minute, then opens the breech. No. 2 extracts the round, and examines the primer.	
		Primer struck	No. 2 shouts "Faulty cartridge—new round."	
		or Primer not struck.	No. 2 shouts "New striker."	
		Gun firing all right.		
21	Detachment commander.	Cease firing.	No. 1 clears the gun. No. 2 depresses the sights. No. 1 swings the barrel round at right angles to the line of fire and applies the brake; then stands on the base wheel and pulls on the apex wheel. (If in the open, he first fixes the loop of a toggle rope to the hub of the apex wheel). The detachment commander and No. 2 prepare to overturn the gun.	When in the open No. 1 should depress the sight himself.
			No. 3 moves off to the trailer, remaining there at ease until the detachment returns.	This represents the return of unexpended ammunition to the trailer.

22	Detachment commander.	Over.	The detachment commander and No. 2 assist No. 1 in overturning the gun (if in the open they pull on the toggle rope, thereby keeping the gun between them and the enemy).	If in the open, smoke, eg SIP Grenades should be used to cover this movement.
23	Detachment commander.	Take post.	The detachment (less No. 3) falls in around the gun.	
24	BAR Group commander.	BAR group—covering fire.	BAR group comes to attention.	This represents fire to cover the detachment out of action.
25	Detachment commander.	Detachment—brake off — advance — double.	The detachment moves (less No. 3) off at the double to the point where the trailer was left.	
26	BAR Group commander.	BAR group — stop —follow me.	BAR group stand at ease, and are led to join the detachment.	
27	Detachment commander. BAR Group commander.	Detachment—halt. BAR group—halt.	The detachment having reached their original positions, but facing in the opposite direction, halts and stands at ease. The BAR group halts and stands at ease as above.	

Serial No.	Word of command given by	Word of command.	Detail—action by detachment and BAR group.	Remarks—what the movement represents.
28	Detachment commander.	Limber up. Take post.	The detachment reconnects the trailer to the gun. The detachment falls in in their correct positions around the gun. The BAR group falls in as in Serial 2.	
29	Detachment commander.	Detachment and BAR group—number.	The detachment and BAR group number as before. Each man states amount of unexpended ammunition he has left and any information gained. Detachment commander then reports — task completed — casualties — ammunition — information—ready to move.	This represents taking stock of casualties, ammunition expended and information gained, also collecting ammunition from casualties and redistributing it. This represents detachment commander reporting to the higher commander and will be done automatically without orders.

APPENDIX E.

CONCEALMENT AND DECEPTION.

1. **Introduction.** Fifty years ago a French dictionary would tell you that a chauffeur stoked a furnace and you would find that the word camouflage is not in the dictionary. It takes an Englishman to invent a Rolls Royce engine, but the English had to adapt a French word for the man who was to drive this superb invention.

Camouflage was a word that became anglicised in the last war and has come to cover two English words, concealment and deception.

In animals, concealment is an instinct arrived at by the survival of the fittest. If the evolution of the animal does not keep pace with changes in its environment, the species dies out. There is nothing more obvious than a sparrow's nest or the eggs it contains. The fecundity of the species allows it to survive all casualties. Probably that is why its concealment is so imperfect. In Britain, however, there is a shortage of manpower, and Home Guard must be less careless (when on active service) than sparrows.

The most ambitious camoufleur has not yet claimed to have developed the epidermic capacities of the chameleon. He can, however, disguise himself and learn to move in surroundings and against backgrounds to achieve the same results. The comparative mental and physical effort each uses is difficult to measure. It has been said that the leopard cannot change his spots. Nor can a soldier conveniently change his camouflage as often as an actor does his costumes. Therefore if the concealed object is to move, the camouflage must fit all the background where it is to be in operation. A town Home Guard sniper's suit will show up in a green field like a boiled lobster back on the sea bottom, and will have about as much chance of living to fight another day.

Of all subjects least susceptible to teaching by lecture, camouflage takes the lead. It is a matter for the eye and is best taught by demonstration and learned by practice. In the Introduction to this Instruction, concealment is given as one of the seven principles of defence. This Appendix includes some notes on concealment and deception for the individual, his weapons and their emplacements. The notes do not attempt to be at all complete and are inserted more to encourage the Home Guard to avail themselves of courses and advice from camouflage officers and lecturers who can be consulted on application to Command camouflage officers or schools, to the GHQ Home Guard Schools and to Command Weapon Training Schools. Concealment and deception are essential to successful fighting because they are the main methods for achieving surprise. But they must be the servants and not the masters of the soldier. The means to deceive must never hamper the free movement of the fighting man and his weapon. It must never be emphasized at the expense of the fighting spirit and of direct attack where necessary.

2. Concealment materials. Various materials and their uses are listed in the Camouflage MTPs. Shortage of shipping space and other results of war preclude issue in any quantities to the Home Guard. Home-made substitutes can often be an improvement on issued material designed for use throughout the world. The Home Guard knows where he is going to fight. He has only to vary the texture and tone of his concealment for the seasons. Materials lie ready to his hand in the salvage dump, his neighbour's chicken run, or where his wife stores the lace curtains. If their use opens a local second front he has the consolation of knowing that it will automatically die down when the invasion balloon goes up.

3. Individual concealment. Vary individual concealment—AVOID REPETITION. Camouflage must be operationally efficient and comfortable.

(*a*) *Skin.* It is of vital importance that all exposed skin should be darkened, even when the face veil is worn. Every Home Guard should carry darkening material on his person. Burnt powdered cork made into a paste with melted fat or vaseline gives fair results, but is shiny and inclined to rub off.

Various firms will now supply an excellent cream, the cost of which may be debited to the Training Grant.

(*b*) *Clothing and equipment.* *See* Fig. 24 and notes.

CLOTHING AND EQUIPMENT CONCEALMENT.

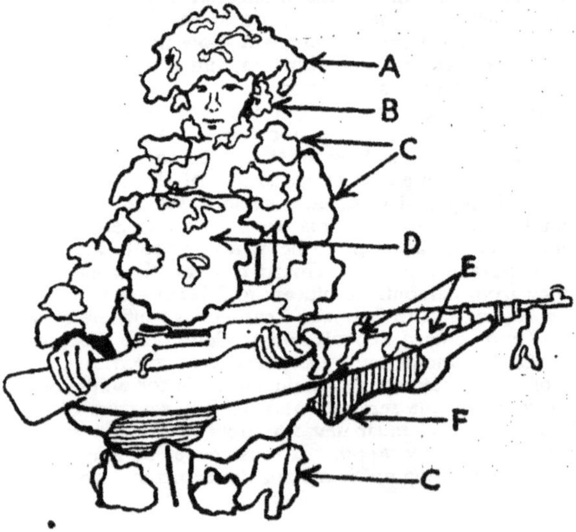

FIG. 24.

NOTES.

A. Shape of helmet broken up by stuffing balls of grass, etc., under net. Scrim tied on to net and dropping over edge.

B. Pieces of scrim, paper, etc., tied on to chin strap.

C. Pieces of rag, scrim, paper, cardboard, etc., tied on to shoulder straps and round arms and legs.

D. Respirator covered with piece of old sandbag cut to irregular shape and tied to sling at top corners, and held on to respirator by passing string right round. Where string passes over side of respirator tie on pieces of scrim to break side surfaces.

NOTE.—There is no need to take sandbag round back of respirator.

E. Pieces of string tied round stock with scrim woven in and out, ends hanging down.

F. False sling of sacking cut to irregular shape—or length of string with bits of suitable salvage tied on, running from piling swivel to lower sling swivel.

Colours for country. Brown and green.

Colours for town and rocky country. Brown, or black and red, or black and two greys (stone and slate).

(c) *Steel helmet.* *See* Fig. 25.

(d) *Boots.* Hide all shine with dubbin.

(e) *The "Sniper Sandal."* (*See* Home Guard Instruction No. 51, Part III.) It should be noted that the method there shown can be used for any material such as old carpet, coconut matting, felt, etc.

(f) "*The Sniper Hood.*" Owing to the shortage of hessian, it is no longer possible to issue it for making sniper suits. If the arms, legs, hands and waist are concealed as described in preceding paragraphs and a sandbag is converted into a sniper hood as detailed below and shown in the Fig. 26, it will be found that a man has more mobility and equal concealment as is obtained from a sniper suit.

Paint sandbag a dirty brownish green.

STEEL HELMET CONCEALMENT.

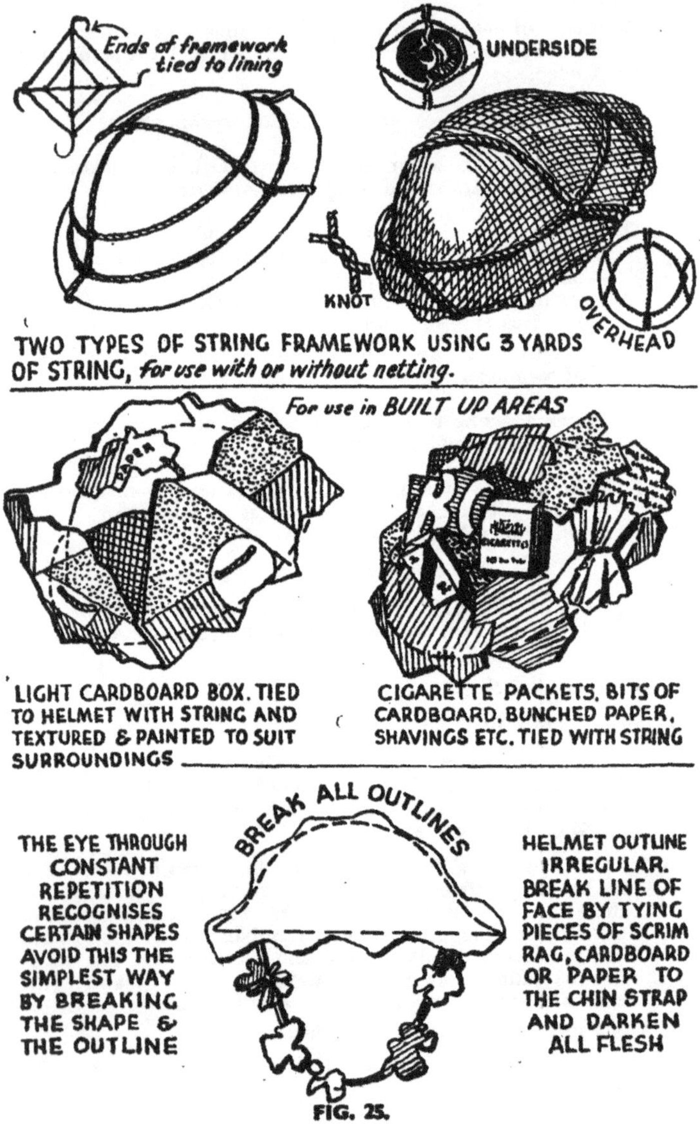

Ends of framework tied to lining
UNDERSIDE
KNOT
OVERHEAD
TWO TYPES OF STRING FRAMEWORK USING 3 YARDS OF STRING, for use with or without netting.
For use in BUILT UP AREAS
PAPER
LIGHT CARDBOARD BOX. TIED TO HELMET WITH STRING AND TEXTURED & PAINTED TO SUIT SURROUNDINGS
CIGARETTE PACKETS, BITS OF CARDBOARD, BUNCHED PAPER, SHAVINGS ETC. TIED WITH STRING
BREAK ALL OUTLINES
THE EYE THROUGH CONSTANT REPETITION RECOGNISES CERTAIN SHAPES AVOID THIS THE SIMPLEST WAY BY BREAKING THE SHAPE & THE OUTLINE
HELMET OUTLINE IRREGULAR. BREAK LINE OF FACE BY TYING PIECES OF SCRIM RAG, CARDBOARD OR PAPER TO THE CHIN STRAP AND DARKEN ALL FLESH

FIG. 25.

Cut the sides of sandbag along seam, and opposite side to seam, until 2 inches from bottom. Hem edges.

Place slit bag on steel helmet so that bottom seam of bag is across top of helmet. Mark area for vision. Withdraw all horizontal threads, and if necessary, alternative vertical threads. Alternatively mark shape of gauze on sandbag, cut hole and sew in gauze (if it is available).

Garnish bag with dark green and dark brown bows of approximately 7 inches long, using half widths of scrim or strips of dyed rag.

Tie four lengths of scrimmed string (for details see below) between the split sides of sandbag so as to conceal the face, neck and shoulders from the side view. The length of the scrimmed string should be adjusted by a second person

IMPROVISED SNIPER'S HOOD.

FIG. 26.

while the sandbag is in position. The scrimmed string should be made just long enough to allow the sandbag to be taken on and off over the steel helmet. The bottom length should be adjusted to slip under armpit.

The scrimmed string should be made as follows :—Tie half-width pieces of garnish 7–8 inches long to thick string. (*See* Fig. 26.)

(*g*) *Shine on glasses.* Avoid by :—

(i) Make fine gauze frame cut to shape and clip over lens.

(ii) Make fringe of hessian, sandbag, curtain netting or raffia (painted) about 18 inches by 6 inches. If hessian or sandbag, draw all horizontal threads to a depth of 4 or 5 inches, leaving an inch or so to tie on to helmet.

4. Concealment of weapon pits.

(*a*) *Tracks.* Paths leading to positions must be joined up to paths in general civilian use. They must not seem to lead into a military position. Make your track plan and see that paths are walked on to keep up the disguise at all times.

(*b*) *Fields of fire.* Don't pin-point a weapon by clearing fan-shaped arcs of fire. Clear to resemble the surrounding landscape.

(*c*) *Spoil.* Remove spoil if you don't conceal it. It can be used to make dummy paths. If it has to be dumped, throw it with other rubbish or in a copse or stream.

(*d*) *Wire.* Wire shows up from the air. Make it follow existing fences, where possible.

(*e*) Dust flies up if ground is dry where a machine gun is firing. Keep the ground wet.

5. Screens. *See* Fig. 27 and 28 for use in the country and in towns.

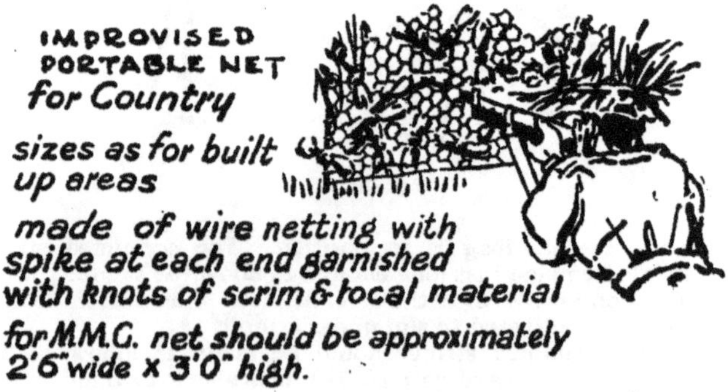
IMPROVISED
PORTABLE NET
for Country
sizes as for built
up areas
made of wire netting with
spike at each end garnished
with knots of scrim & local material
for M.M.G. net should be approximately
2'6" wide x 3'0" high.

FIG. 27.

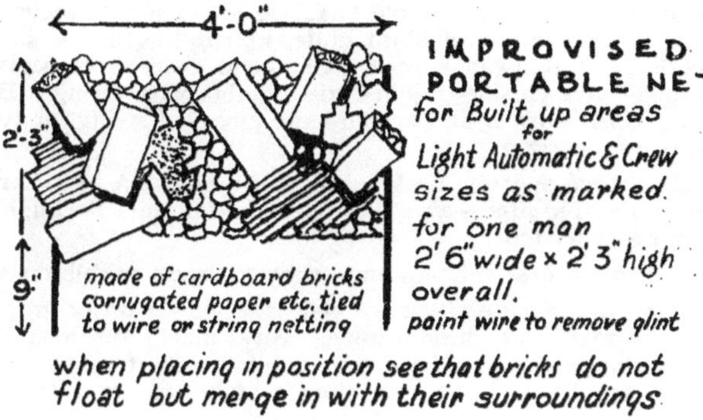
4'-0"
IMPROVISED PORTABLE NET
for Built up areas for Light Automatic & Crew
sizes as marked.
for one man
2' 6" wide × 2' 3" high
overall.
paint wire to remove glint
2'-3"
9"
made of cardboard bricks
corrugated paper etc. tied
to wire or string netting
when placing in position see that bricks do not
float but merge in with their surroundings

FIG. 28.

6. **Imitation bricks**

(*a*) See Fig. 29

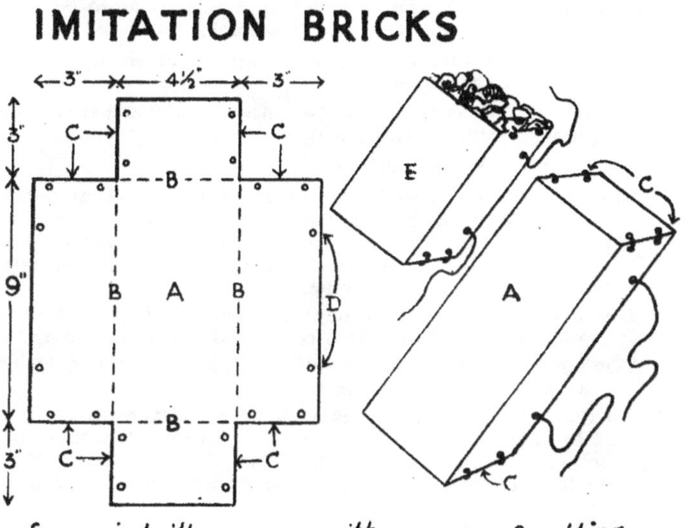

FIG. 29.

Take a piece of cardboard or old box. A cut to size 15 inches by 10½ inches, score a line with blunt knife, knitting needle or awl at B for bending. Cut away corners at C, bend away from scoring. Bore two holes at each side of join C, tie together with string. Bore two holes at open sides D and attach loose pieces of string for tying on to weapon or netting

For half or three-quarters broken bricks E make as A but shorten to whatever size required—at either one or both ends tie bunched paper, paint and flatten.

Paint to suit natural surrounding—such as brick rubble on site.

Colours to use are generally brick red splashed cream or grey (to represent mortar) and dark brown. Any matt, bitumistic or emulsified paint will do. These are to some extent water-proof. Texture can be obtained, by sprinkling a little sand or brick-dust with paint.

(*b*) Figs. 30 and 31 show a sniper and a 29 mm. spigot mortar concealed in a blitzed town area using cardboard bricks.

7. **Dummy positions.** The object of dummy positions is to divert the enemy's attention from the real ones; to draw his fire and waste ammunition; and to direct his attack as as to be most vulnerable to the defence and to counter-attack.

Therefore when planning dummy positions and siting dummy weapons and tanks remember :—

(*a*) Dummy positions must not be closer than 200 yards from occupied or alternative positions.

(*b*) They must be realistically sited.

(*c*) They must be made to appear alive. Fresh tracks, an occasional small fire and some movement in quiet moments will help to achieve this. In battle, dummies may be used and an occasional shot should be fired from such positions. Don't let them appear derelict.

(*d*) Dummy trenches need not be dug to the full depth. A very shallow slit will look like a completed one from the air.

(*e*) Don't forget to add a bit of defensive wire and clear fields of fire, etc. Such things help realism.

(*f*) To fool the enemy, dummies must be well planned, carefully co-ordinated and well prepared. Obvious dummies will only draw attention to the fact that an area is held. Well made dummies will prevent the enemy seeing how it is held.

Dummy road-blocks. **Enemy tanks can not only be delayed but can often be forced off their route and diverted into a pre-selected killing ground by a cunning use of dummy road-blocks.**

FIG. 31.
29-MM. SPIGOT MORTAR CONCEALED IN A TOWN.

FIG. 30.
SNIPER CONCEALED IN A TOWN.

8. Sub-artillery concealment.

(*a*) *Concealment of the* **3-*inch OSB*** *gun* (*Smith Gun*). Prepared positions. (*See* **Figs. 32 and 33.**)

(i) *The weapon.* The chief points which render this weapon conspicuous are :—

The silhouette of the gun.

Solution. Site close to a suitable background.

The shine from the upturned disc wheels when the gun is in action.

Solution. Paint wheels with matt camouflage paint S.C.C., No. 1A dark brown or S.C.C., No. 14 black). If possible, add texture in form of grit or shavings to wheels with an adhesive substance before painting. Connect up holes near the rim of the wheels with wires in order to allow garnish in the form of local rubbish or branches to be inserted, covering the wheel and protruding over its edge.

The shine and shape of the gun-shield.

Solution. Paint as above. Wires may be attached across the shield at either side of the gun-slit. They may be used to support garnish in a similar way to the wires on the wheels. Sandbags placed on top of the gun should be darkened, and made to imitate rubbish. Small pieces of curtain net, well garnished with tufts of rubbish, can be of great use when used over the wheels or can be supported at either side of the gun-shield by a strong wire temporarily clamped to the shield when the gun is in action.

(ii) *The limber*—which presents much the same problem as the gun.

Solution. Paint and wire top wheel as above. Paint also all metal surfaces.

NOTE.—*Concealment of the limber will normally be effected by placing it at a slight distance behind cover.*

(iii) *Personal concealment.* Personal concealment of the gun crew must be given due attention. Small wire screens garnished with foliage or rubbish can be used to give good concealment from either flank.

In hasty positions concealment is extremely difficult and the crew will depend for safety mainly upon quick occupation, firing one or two rounds and moving to another position. At short range the crest clearance will make firing over cover impossible, wherever possible, a defiladed position should be selected.

FIG. 32.
3-INCH OSB GUN—BEFORE CONCEALMENT

FIG. 33.
3-INCH OSB GUN—AFTER CONCEALMENT

(*b*) *The Spigot Mortar.* As the Spigot Mortar is a short range weapon, effective concealment of the mortar, trench and personnel s essential Good siting is of the utmost importance.

Concealment from ground view should be the main aim, *even if the field of fire is thereby reduced.*

Concealment from air view should, however, not be neglected.

POSITION.

(i) *Ground view.* To obtain concealment, the position should, wherever possible, be dug close to a natural background. Weapon, crew and movement will then be easier to conceal.

If the position is without an immediate natural background, an artificial one must be made. Where possible, natural materials should be used and placed on the edge of the circular trench in an uneven line behind and at the sides of the 180 degrees traverse. In those cases where a 360 degree traverse is required, the artificial background must be so constructed as to be capable of immediate removal

Cut feathered netting (cullacorts) attached to rabbit or revetting wire is an excellent and lasting substitute for natural foliage or brushwood. Sticks or iron rods of suitable length can be stuck into the ground as upright supports for material and are instantly removable. A screen, 6 inches high, of the same material can be placed along the front of the trench. This will assist in hiding movement of the crew.

Except in special cases all spoil should be removed from the site. (*See* Figs. **34** and **35**.)

(ii) *Air view.* Light covers can be used to break up the shape from air view of slit trenches and weapon pit. They must be instantly removable wherever necessary when the position is occupied and hidden under cover from ground view. Branches will serve if made up covers are not available. Steel wool attached to a rough frame is recommended, if cut in an irregular shape.

Steel wool will also be useful for covering a communication trench and for temporarily hiding bare earth round the weapon pit. The concrete pillar and sides of pit should be darkened, and the former textured on top. (*See* **Fig. 36.**)

FIG. 34.
29-MM. SPIGOT MORTAR—BEFORE CONCEALMENT

FIG. 35.
29-MM. SPIGOT MORTAR—AFTER CONCEALMENT

29-MM. SPIGOT MORTAR—AIR CONCEALMENT†

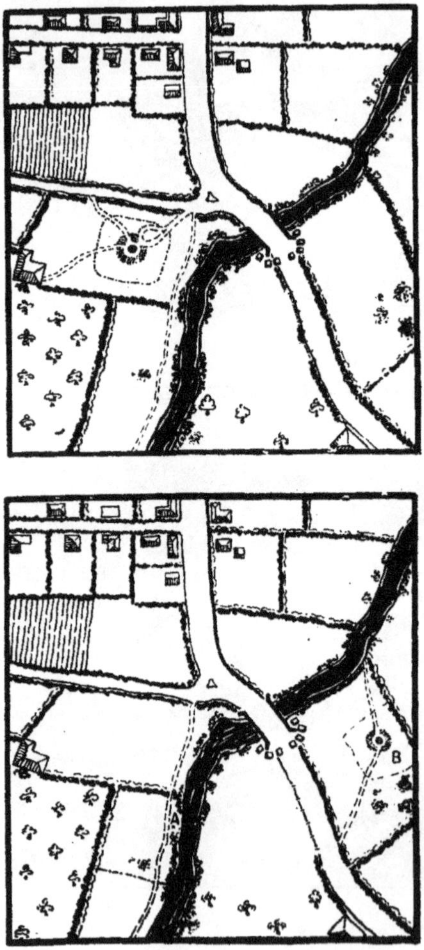

WRONG

SPIGOT MORTAR in prepared position. Position revealed by signs of activity.
TRACKS converge pointing to position vehicles make turning loop.
SPOIL shows up light, framing position.
WIRE protecting wire causes dark patch of long grass.
CONCRETE pillar and revetment shine.
REASON:—BADLY SITED

RIGHT

SPIGOT MORTAR correctly sited A.
TRACKS. Where possible use existing tracks or make false tracks appear natural (a track plan is vital).
SPOIL. Remove from position cleanly can be spread on track or used to make false track.
WIRE. Protecting wire should conform to normal ground pattern.
CONCRETE must be rough cast and painted.
Road blocks are usually impossible to hide.
Enemy reconnaissance planes will search for the positions of covering weapons. Conceal the real position and erect a dummy to give false information
Dummy position B shows suggestion of track planning, bu actual position is indifferently concealed—use track occasionally to give impression of occupation.
Remember 90 per cent. of good concealment is SITING and DISCIPLINE

FIG. 36.

MORTAR.

(iii) The design of this mortar creates certain definite shadows: if necessary these can to a large extent be eliminated by painting the upper half of the concave side of the shield with a light straw coloured oil paint, adding occasional patches of dark green. The under half of the cylinder and the interior of the latter should also be painted a light straw colour (this is known as counter-shading).

(iv) The square shape of the shield can be distorted by additions of artificial materials. Four ⅜-inch holes may be drilled in the corners of the shield to facilitate attachment of material. The material may be allowed to hang over the sides of the shield.

(v) The bomb and muzzle of the cylinder are very conspicuous from ground view at short range, and must be effectively concealed in order to ensure the element of *surprise* for the first shot of any series. A feather-weight cover should be devised to attach over the bomb up to the muzzle of the cylinder and in general should be a green colour. No cover must weigh more than a few ounces and must not interfere with sighting. Tow, B.G. fabric or light natural garnish are suitable materials. *See* Figs. 35 and 37 for concealment in country and Figs. 31 and 38 for concealment in towns.

- 29 MM SPIGOT MORTAR - CONCEALMENT METHOD IN COUNTRY -

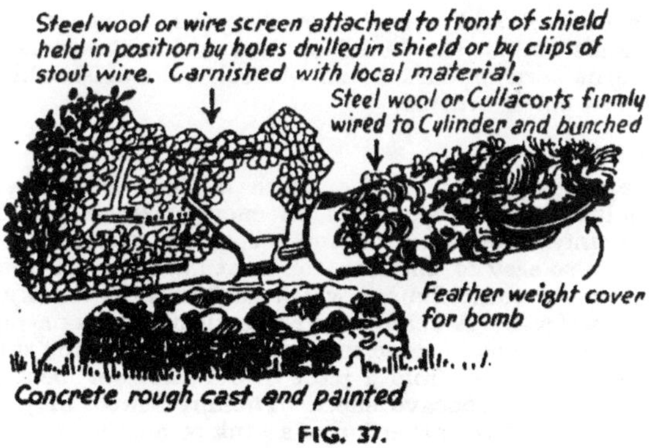

FIG. 37.

SPIGOT MORTAR
Built up area Concealment
Wire frame attached to shield garnished with cardboard-bricks, cardboard or sacking painted to suit background
Heaps of brick rubble should be distributed around to complete the picture & to give natural appearance from both air & ground
Cylinder opening masked by stretching paper or sacking across & tied lightly round lip. Incised from rim edge to centre. allows free access of bomb & falls back into place after discharge. Piece of stiff paper stuck on nose of bomb.
NOTE:- THE ABOVE METHOD IS SUITABLE FOR BOTH TOWN & COUNTRY. USING MATERIALS TO SUIT BACKGROUND

FIG. 38.

29-MM. SPIGOT MORTAR—BUILT-UP AREA CONCEALMENT.

PERSONNEL.

(vi) The crew should wear sniper disguises to waist level and hands and wrists should be darkened with special cream, burnt cork or dark green blanco. Gloves should not be worn unless ordered.

DECEPTION.

(vii) Use any ingenious device which might have the effect of halting or slowing down an enemy vehicle (eg. screens, dummy mines, etc.). Dummy spigot mortars and positions are also easy to simulate, the most important feature being simply dummy figures, which need only be constructed to waist level. A suitable sized earthenware drain-pipe or a bomb case make good dummy cylinders and the shield can be constructed from a piece of old linoleum, bent slightly to give the concave effect. Dummy smoke may successfully divert the attention of a tank commander.

(*c*) *The Northover Projector.*

(i) This is a short range weapon requiring careful, but simple, concealment. The following method is recommended :—

The weapon should be sited well into a natural background.

The white metal back sight should be darkened with either dark brown (S.C.C. No. 1A) or dark green (S.C.C. No. 7) paint. An oil bound paint of either colour is preferable.

Unless the barrel is well under cover its shape should be distorted with either :—

Garnished string (*see* 3-inch OSB gun) with artificial or natural garnish.

Steel wool (green) or tufts of natural foliage secured to barrel at approximately 3-inch intervals by rubber bands, string or wire.

Muzzle. The shadow of the muzzle is visible at short range, but this can be hidden by a piece of cullacorts suspended over the muzzle. *No. 2 must remove this material before firing.* To enable him to do so, without unnecessary movement, a length of wire can be attached to the cullacorts and carried down the side of the barrel. The end of the wire should be attached to the handle.

NOTE.—*When using any of the above materials care must be taken to avoid obscuring the line of sight.*

Legs of tripod should be hidden by :—

Screen of rabbit wire with cullacorts or garnish inserted.

Small garnished garden net (knot garnish, half width). Short brushwood or natural foliage stick into ground in natural manner to a height which will not interfere with the traversing of the barrel.

Garnished string wrapped round each leg.

Crew to wear sniper disguises to waist and keep as still as possible.

Skin to be darkened.

(ii) In towns, different camouflage materials must be used. Fig. 39 shows a Northover and crew with bricks cut away to show gun and crew in a blitzed area.

NORTHOVER PROJECTOR CONCEALED IN
TOWN AREA.

FIG. 39.

NOTES.—

(i) Figure shows Northover in " blitzed " ground—crew concealed using salvage materials such as painted cardboard, bunched brown paper tied together with odd pieces of string, faces darkened, chin straps garnished with bits of cardboard and paper to break outline of face. Cardboard brick tied to barrel and on legs. No. 3 acting as protection.

(ii) Concealment from air view will in most cases be possible by siting under natural cover. When this is not possible all conspicuous and suspicious objects (eg. wooden SIP boxes) should be placed under cover. The gun crew should " freeze."

(2872.) 34992. Wt. 33671-2155. 330M. 11/43. A., P. & S., Ltd. 428.

www.ingramcontent.com/pod-product-compliance
Lightning Source LLC
LaVergne TN
LVHW091308080426
835510LV00007B/419
9781843425755